Traveling Abroad for Life and Work

Traveling Abroad for Life and Work

Julia Pennyworth

MURPHY & MOORE
www.murphy-moorepublishing.com

Traveling Abroad for Life and Work
Julia Pennyworth
ISBN: 978-1-63987-807-9 (Hardback)

Ⓜ MURPHY & MOORE

Murphy & Moore Publishing
1 Rockefeller Plaza,
New York City,
NY 10020, USA

Cataloging-in-Publication Data

Traveling abroad for life and work / Julia Pennyworth.
      p. cm.
Includes bibliographical references and index.
ISBN 978-1-63987-807-9
1. Travel--Guidebooks. 2. Voyages and travels. 3. Tourism--Management. I. Pennyworth, Julia.
G153.4 .T73 2023
910.202--dc23

Table of Contents

Preface

Traveling has a profound influence on both the personal and professional fronts of an individual as it acts as a mode of learning some essential life skills such as the ability to adapt, better communication skills, teamwork, cultural awareness, performing within constraints, leadership and time management. All these traits are also the characteristics of an entrepreneur and a successful businessperson. Today, there are avenues for business travel that integrates leisure and work for the busy professional. A focused avenue of tourism that targets this section of travelers is business tourism. Business tours include work-related activities such as attending meetings and conferences, inspections and consultations, as well as leisure activities such as sightseeing, recreation, dining out, etc. Such tours and travels also accommodate larger groups, for conferences and conventions, exhibitions and trade fairs. This textbook provides innovative insights into the practice of traveling abroad for business and pleasure. It provides a step-by-step guide on the ways to arrange and manage business tours. It will serve as a complete reference text to travelers, tour managers and all professionals involved in the industry of tourism and travel.

To facilitate a deeper understanding of the contents of this book a short introduction of every chapter is written below:

Chapter 1- Traveling has many benefits for the mind as well as the body. It can improve general health, cure anxiety and depression, break monotony, give exposure to new cultures, traditions and languages, new cuisines, etc. This chapter introduces in brief about traveling abroad for work or leisure and the way to pay when in a different country.

Chapter 2- Business travel is undertaken for work or professional reasons. During business travel, an individual may attend conferences, exhibitions, and meetings. Dining out, recreation, sightseeing and shopping can also be a part of business travel, depending on convenience. This chapter has been carefully written to provide an overview of business traveling and addresses the various aspects of traveling in business class, booking a hotel room, getting discounts on a business class ticket and preparing for an important meeting while abroad.

Chapter 3- Planning a travel budget and calculating the finance required for a tour or vacation is vital to traveling. Expenses may vary greatly depending on the form of transportation, accommodation or food one opts for. Further, sightseeing tours, museum fees, recreational activity prices, etc. also need to be considered while planning a travel budget. The topics elaborated in this chapter on traveling on a limited budget, exchanging currency and getting the best exchange rates in a country, using travel vouchers, finding travel discounts, etc. are aimed at providing innovative insights into travel budgeting and finances.

Chapter 4- There are various strategies for having a fruitful and exhilarating travel experience. This chapter provides some useful tips for traveling, such as the correct way to pack for air travel, dress for travel, find cheap accommodation, talk with someone speaking a different language, interact with people from different cultures, etc.

Chapter 5- Traveling the world requires careful planning, scheduling and budgeting. This chapter is a comprehensive guide on world travel. It addresses some important ways to make traveling across the globe including South America, Canada, United States, Germany, Switzerland and the UK an easy task.

Finally, I would like to thank the entire team involved in the inception of this book for their valuable time and contribution. This book would not have been possible without their efforts. I would also like to thank my friends and family for their constant support.

Julia Pennyworth

Traveling Abroad

Traveling has many benefits for the mind as well as the body. It can improve general health, cure anxiety and depression, break monotony, give exposure to new cultures, traditions and languages, new cuisines, etc. This chapter introduces in brief about traveling abroad for work or leisure and the way to pay when in a different country.

How to Travel Abroad

Traveling abroad can be a strikingly simple endeavor when you're prepared. Do your research and study the destination; plan your itinerary and arrange the logistics; and pack for the weather, culture, and activities that you expect. Read on for more specific tips on successfully traveling abroad.

Method 1. Researching a Destination

1. Do your research. You need to research where you are going, the flight times and prices for airlines, and which documents you need to take with you. Plan out your itinerary carefully. Some cities, like London or Paris, really need a week to see what they have to offer. Travel times also need to be taken into consideration. Traveling by train can take longer than traveling by car.

2. Get a good guidebook. Fodor's, Rick Steves, and the Michelin guides are all excellent places to start. Make sure you have the most up-to-date guide book for the area of the world you intend to visit. Some are updated every year. Others are updated every other year, or every few years. A good guidebook is a $15-20 investment that can save a lot of headache.

- Don't be afraid to rip it up and staple together only the pieces you need. A well-kept guide-book might make a nice souvenir, but it may not be worth the extra weight of carrying around information that you don't need.

3. Understand the basic customs of the area. Before going on the trip, research what is and is not acceptable in your destination. When you arrive, observe how others act in person. Remember: some things are okay for locals to do, but not for tourists to do.

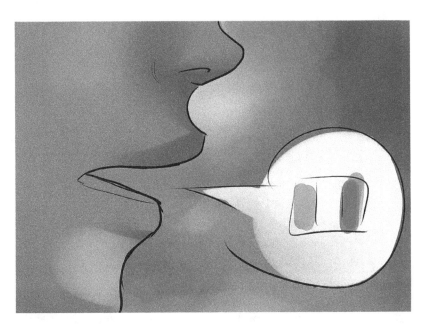

4. Learn some basic phrases of the country you are going to. This is just polite. Even if you struggle with it, the locals will appreciate that you've at least tried their language instead of rudely asking "Do you speak English?" (Or whatever your native tongue happens to be.) If you use the native language to ask for something, expect the reply to be in that language and at normal conversational speed – which is going to be faster than the audio lessons you learned. This is not to say that you shouldn't learn some basic greetings and questions. You should, however, be ready for the responses.

5. Get a reliable map of the area you are going to. Memorize it and note each of the places you will be visiting. Keep your map safe and dry. If you have access to a laptop or a smartphone (with data), you may not expressly need a physical map – but it is still usually smart to carry one as a backup.

6. Be aware of common scams in your destination. Examples include the "dropped ring" scam, the "fake petition," and friendship bracelets tied on your wrist by aggressive vendors. Also be aware of other common crimes, especially pickpocketing. TSA approved travel locks and money belts are both helpful, especially in areas where pickpocketing is extremely common.

- The infamous #64 bus in Rome, for instance, is popular with pickpockets because it's the only bus in Rome that hits all of the popular tourist destinations. It's usually packed with tourists, and thick with thieves.

- Know what each local coin and bill is worth. For example, in Panama, everything is tied to the US dollar, so money comes in the same size, denomination, and material. In the UK, you'll find 1p, 2p, 5p, 10p, 20p, 50p, £1, and £2 coins, as well as 5, 10, 20, and 50 pound notes. By knowing your denominations and specifying how much you are handing over, you can help avoid another common scam: intentionally incorrect change.

Method 2. Planning your Itinerary

1. Prepare your travel documents. Make sure your passport is up to date and won't expire be-

fore your trip ends. Different countries have different requirements for passports and visas, but in general, your passport should not expire less than 6 months after your expected return date.

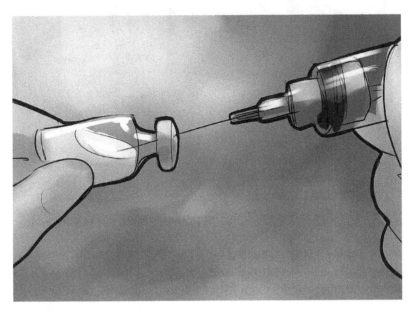

2. Look into vaccine requirements. The country you're going to may require you to have certain vaccines up to date. Make an appointment with your doctor to get this taken care of, as well as other medical considerations.

3. Get travel insurance. Check you have the appropriate cover, and look into international health insurance. Chances are that you will never fall ill while traveling abroad, but it has happened. Bones have been broken; people have gotten food poisoning; pregnant women previously cleared for travel have gone into premature labor. Consider whether the added expense is worth being "safe rather than sorry".

4. Decide where you're going to stay. Housing choices are largely a matter of budget, comfort, and convenience. You can pay for a private hotel room or share a hostel; stay with friends or family; or explore online travel communities like Couchsurfing.com, AirBnB, or WWOOF.org.

- Think about staying in an apartment if you'll be in one place for more than half a week. Hotels can be expensive, and you can often get much better deals for renting out someone's house. Furthermore, this approach might give you a more authentic idea of what it's like to live in a given city.

- Consider a Bed and Breakfast or a self-service vacation rental. This last type of accommodation can help save money, as they're often cheaper than hotels, and you'll save money by buying your groceries and cooking there instead of going out to eat.

5. Figure out how you're going to get around. Your options are broad and varied, and you'll have to choose the best mode of transportation to suit your itinerary. If you will be traveling long distances

between destinations, you might consider flying or taking trains. If you'll be traveling within a city or region, try biking, renting a car, or using public transportation. Research the place you're going and try to understand how the locals get around.

- Trains can be relaxing over long distances. Consider taking night trains – in theory, you can sleep on the train and awake as the train pulls into your next destination.

- If you plan to rent a car, look into insurance requirements. Consider applying for your international driver's license.

- Ferries are a solid option for crossing water. They are usually cheaper than another plane ticket, with better food.

6. Don't take animals, plants or anything else that's not accepted on flights. If you plan to travel with your pets, look at the rules and regulations for traveling with them to keep them out of quarantine. This generally includes a certificate of health from your vet, making sure that rabies vaccines are up to date, having them microchipped, and even a certificate of health from your local government office, such as the Department of Agriculture in the U.S.

Method 3. Packing Effectively

1. Make a list a few weeks before the trip. The list should include everything you are going to take with you. You can put these items into separate columns under what bag they are going in. If you

don't have everything you need, write it down then buy it when you are shopping, this way you can prepare everything so you are organised.

- If you are still struggling with what to pack, you can find an online rough guide with the essentials and basics. When you are all packed, take out you passport and any other travelling documents and keep them with you in a separate bag with your purse and phone, so it all stays together.

2. Pack efficiently. No matter how you're traveling, extra bags and unnecessary things will weigh you down. As travel writer Rick Steves says, "You can't travel happy, heavy, and cheap. Pick two."

- A few classic pieces that are easily mixed and matched and a knowledge of how to use the local laundromat can save you money on overweight baggage fees.

- Know the common dress codes for your destination. For example, if you're visiting the Vatican, women will need their shoulders covered.

3. Research airline regulations for what you can pack. If you're flying, you don't want to exceed the maximum weight. Extra or overweight bags often cost more money, and most airlines don't allow carry-on bags over a certain weight.

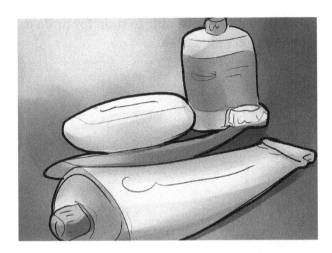

4. Consider leaving basic toiletries behind. You don't have to take everything you think you'll need. Nearly every country you'll visit will have basics like toothpaste, deodorant, soap, and contact solution, and you can't carry more than an three ounces of any liquid in carry on luggage, anyway. Carry copies of your prescriptions in case you run out.

How to Work and Travel

Do you want to travel but still earn money while you're on the road? This dream is becoming a reality for many people, especially as the Internet makes it possible to work from anywhere and has increased our awareness of job opportunities abroad. There are two main types of jobs you can get to help you travel and work at the same time – travel-based jobs, meaning you have to travel to get to or to do the job; and travel freedom jobs, meaning you can do the job from anywhere. With a little effort and hard work you can get the kind of job that lets you travel and work at the same time.

Method 1. Getting a Travel-Based Job

1. Get a travel industry job. What skills do you have that you could use while traveling? Some

employers have seasonal work that you may be able to train for or do easily. Research online and you will find travel-based jobs for every kind of skill.

2. Become an adventure guide. Adventure outfitters and summer camps recruit guides in the off season. If you want to be a rafting guide in the USA, start looking for summer work in the autumn or winter.

- Surf instructors in Costa Rica work during the winters.

- Make a travel plan and network with other guides who can provide job information.

- Resorts need staff for every activity they offer, so find out things you can do at your skill level.

3. Get a job as a nurse. Traveling nurses are in high demand. Many agencies will hire nurses from three months to a year to work at hospitals around the USA. Some even offer housing. Search on-line for traveling nursing positions and contact the recruiters. Most websites list location, pay rate, and benefits up front.

4. Become a travel professional. Airline pilots, flight attendants, cruise ship staff, and transportation employees such as truck drivers travel as part of their work. While some of these jobs don't allow for much time to explore tourist areas, travel professionals can find ways to get out and enjoy, too. Research the industry to see what kind of skills and training are required.

5. Try teaching English abroad. There are many opportunities to teach English abroad. Most places require that you take their Test of English as a Foreign Language (TOEFL) training class before you can sign on. This may expensive, but once you have the TOEFL certification, you can teach in many countries. Agencies often help with job placement.

6. Get a service industry job. Many tourist destinations have resorts, theme parks, and restaurants

looking for waiters, housekeepers, and attendants. The highest seasons for family tourist destinations are when children are not in school. For other places, high season may be during the best weather or centered around holidays. Check around for vacation high season in the area where you want to travel.

Method 2. Earning Income with the Freedom to Travel

1. Get a freelance job. Many writers, photographers, web designers, and graphic designers can do their work from anywhere in the world as long as they have an Internet connection. There are online companies recruiting people with these types of skills. Be wary of anyone asking for money. There are plenty of legitimate companies hiring freelancers. Be prepared to bid for freelance work or possibly get paid a bit less than if you worked in the same job at an office.

2. Start working from home. Ask your current employer if you might be able to start working from home (if that's possible for your type of work). If they say yes, then you may be able to start traveling and completing your work while you're on the road. Most work-from-home jobs allow

employees to complete the bulk of their work online or to submit their work from another location. You don't have to *stay* home to *work* from home.

3. Figure out how to earn passive income. If you have web design and writing skills, you may start blogs or content-based websites that generate passive income through advertising and referral programs. This takes a bit of a time investment upfront, but once the site is established and active, it may generate returns. Start these sites while traveling or better yet, get them up and running before you go. Sites that are generating money will need maintenance and content updates once you are on the road.

- Advertisers usually make direct deposits into your bank account. Depending on your home country, there may be restrictions or limitations to getting paid, so be sure you have access to the money you earn before you begin your travels.

4. Start your own business. Become a travel consultant, importer, or zip-line installer. Find a need for your specific services and skills, then market them in a way that makes sense for you and gives you the freedom you desire from your work.

- For example, engineers might start a business building zip-lines or obstacle courses for resorts around the world. Travel buffs can offer their services to corporations sending employees on international travel. If you love to shop, set up an importing business and next time you travel get inventory for resale.

Method 3. Learning to Live with Less

1. Get rid of the material excess in your life. This includes things that take up space and cost money. People who successfully work and travel are usually comfortable with living light rather than being loaded down with possessions. If you have an expensive car that requires expensive insurance, you will be required to always make money to pay for that car. Having less possessions means you have more freedom to make enough to live and travel as you like.

2. Downsize your home. Living in a large home was a huge part of the American Dream for so long, but now more and more people are realizing the benefits of inhabiting smaller spaces. The smaller the space is, the less room you have for excessive material possessions too, so it will aid you in the whole process of downsizing your life.

- Living in a smaller home means less maintenance for you, less stress about the upkeep of your home, and probably less money each month in rent or mortgage.

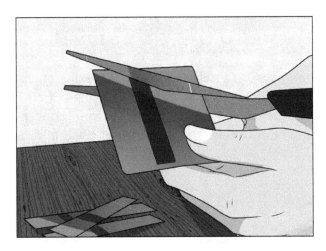

3. Eliminate your debt. Having the freedom to travel because of learning to live with less often means getting rid of your financial ties to your current home location. It is much easier to travel freely when you don't have a mortgage, credit card debt, or a car payment weighing you down and always pulling you back home.

- Try to limit your spending on frivolous luxuries so that you can put some extra money toward your debt each month. This will help you pay it off sooner so you can have more freedom to travel.

- If you plan on traveling for extended periods of time, it might even make sense to sell some of your possessions in order to pay your debts down. For example, if you wanted to move abroad for a while, you might sell your car (since you won't be using it anyways) to help you get your debt to a manageable level.

4. Change your expectations. We live in a consumer culture that is obsessed with always looking for the next big thing – the newest car, the biggest house, the nicest clothes, etc. If you maintain these kinds of expectations and desires for your life, it will be hard for you to be satisfied by living with less.

- Work on realizing that happiness isn't achieved through material possessions and that living with less might help you create a more sustainable, more enjoyable life.

- But to make this work, you'll need to let go of those old expectations.

How to Pay when Traveling Abroad

Traveling to a foreign country can be a rich and rewarding experience. However, one of the biggest hassles in international travel often ends up being figuring out how to pay for things abroad. Foreign transaction and conversion fees are often hidden, while conversion rates for cash are not always straightforward. By planning ahead on using credit cards and cash in cost-effective ways, spending abroad can be as simple and painless as spending at home.

Method 1. Using a Credit Card

1. Call your credit card company to confirm your card can be used abroad. Although credit cards have become increasingly popular around the world over the last few decades, not all credit cards are equally universal. Make sure your card is accepted in your travel destination before departing on your trip.

   - Visa and MasterCard are the most widely accepted credit cards. If your primary card is not from one of these companies, confirm it can be used abroad or consider applying for a card with a new company.

2. Use a card that doesn't have foreign transaction fees. Most credit cards include fees for making

transactions abroad, which range from 2% to 3% of each purchase. If your primary card has such penalties, apply for a new card that doesn't include foreign transaction fees.

- Bank cards are significantly more likely than credit union cards to charge foreign transaction fees. 91% of bank cards charge such fees, while only 57% of credit union cards do so.

- Capital One and Discover do not charge foreign transaction fees on any of their credit cards. Consider these companies for your international travel card.

- Many credit cards also come with travel rewards like free airline miles or credit for making purchases abroad. Consider using a card with travel rewards (e.g., Capital One Ventures Rewards Card) to enjoy even more benefits from traveling abroad.

- Use a card that also doesn't charge currency conversion fees, if possible.

3. Make sure your credit card is secured with an EMV chip. EMV (Europay, MasterCard, and Visa) chips are normally required in most countries and are widely used, especially in Europe. If your card doesn't contain an EMV chip, it may not work in your destination country.

- While most chip cards used in the United States require verification during transactions with a signature, many overseas merchants only accept chip-enabled cards that use PIN verification. Ask your card company about getting a PIN for your card if it doesn't already have one.

- EMV chip-enabled cards are also more secure than traditional mag stripe credit cards, and so are a safer card option for international travelers.

4. Decline currency conversion offers to avoid incurring large fees. Overseas merchants may offer to

show you a bill in your native currency rather than local currency. While this makes calculating the relative cost of an item easier for international travelers, it also adds an extra conversion fee to your bill.

- For example, if you're an American shopping in a souvenir store in a foreign country, the merchant may offer to show you the bill for the items you want to buy in dollars instead of in the local currency.

- This process is called Dynamic Currency Conversion (DCC). Merchants are required to ask you before using DCC, so you should only worry about this process if the offer is made to you.

- Your credit card company will likely charge you a currency conversion fee for your purchase. However, in most instances, the fee charged by your company will be less than the cost associated with accepting a DCC offer.

5. Bring a backup card. The painful reality of international travel is that there's a good chance you might lose personal items to theft or misplacement. Make sure to pack a backup credit card to use in case your primary card is lost or stolen.

- Make sure your backup card is also accepted in your destination country.

- Don't carry both cards on your person at the same time. Leave your backup credit card in a safe location in your hotel room, such as shoved deep underneath your mattress or taped to the bottom of a drawer.

Method 2. Using Local Currency

1. Bring enough converted currency to last the first 24 hours of your trip. Use this money to tide

you over until you can reach an ATM or for immediate expenses after your flight, such as eating at the airport or taking a taxi to your hotel.

2. Convert your cash at a local bank if they offer a good conversion rate. Whether this is a good idea will depend on the conversion rate your bank offers. Large national banks, such as Bank of America, Wells Fargo, Chase, and CitiBank, offer cheaper rates than most other conversion services.

- If you're not a customer of one of these banks, or if they do not have branches in your area, consider waiting until you arrive at your destination airport to convert the rest of your cash.

- Avoid exchanging your money at exchange desks or kiosks. These are far more likely to charge you higher conversion rates than your bank or airport ATMs.

3. Pack a debit card that doesn't charge ATM withdrawal fees. You'll most likely want to use cash for purchases from time to time, so you'll need to bring a debit card you can use to withdraw cash from local ATMs. Call your bank to confirm you won't be charged a fee when using your debit card abroad.

- If your bank applies a fee to using your debit card abroad, consider opening an account at a new bank.

- The most common charges applied to debit card users at foreign ATMs include withdrawal fees, a fee for using an out-of-network ATM, and foreign transaction fees. Make sure your debit card won't incur these charges to save the most money abroad.

- You can avoid many ATM fees by only using ATMs associated with your bank. Find out where the closest bank ATMs are to your hotel after you arrive at your destination.

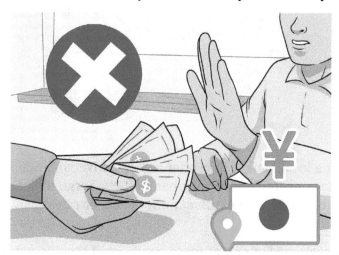

4. Avoid paying in your native currency instead of local cash. Some merchants will advertise that they accept dollars as well as local money to attract American tourists. However, purchases made in dollars in these stores will often cost extra due to hidden exchange rates.

- The same is true if paying with euros in non-eurozone countries like Switzerland and the United Kingdom.

- A convenient way to avoid this situation is to only carry local currency on your person, in addition to a credit card, when going out in a foreign country.

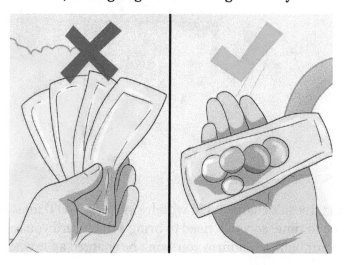

5. Carry small amounts of cash on your person. This will help you avoid losing all of your money

if you are robbed or lose your wallet while abroad. Limiting the amount of cash you carry will also help you to moderate your spending during your time abroad.

- Many smaller shops and stores in some countries may only accept cash instead of credit cards. Having some cash on you at all times will also help you avoid the predicament of making a purchase somewhere that won't take your card

CHAPTER 2
Business Traveling

Business travel is undertaken for work or professional reasons. During business travel, an individual may attend conferences, exhibitions and meetings. Dining out, recreation, sightseeing and shopping can also be a part of business travel, depending on convenience. This chapter has been carefully written to provide an overview of business traveling and addresses the various aspects of traveling in business class, booking a hotel room, getting discounts on a business class ticket and preparing for an important meeting while abroad.

Business Travel

Business travel is a journey specifically taken for work purposes and doesn't include daily commutes, leisure trips or holidays.

According to the WTO (World Trade Organization) around 30 per cent of international trips these days are for business – and business travel shows no sign of slowing down. Even in this world of instant communication and social media, business travel is as necessary and advantageous as ever.

Main Reasons for Business Travel

- Networking. A handshake followed by a face-to-face chat is still the best way to meet and get to know someone – much better than Skype calls or reading dozens of emails and text messages. You may also want to personally show your leadership skills.

- Examples & samples. You may need to take examples or samples of your work or see examples or samples of something you're considering investing in. Explaining something – such as a product or service you offer – while with someone and actually seeing they understand is much better than any other way.

- Be personal. You want to meet suppliers, customers or clients to take them for drinks and a meal and personally give them a gift as a way of showing your gratitude. You want to show them that they are worth the time that it takes to make a personal visit.

- Check conditions. You prefer to visit suppliers to see everything looks fine. For example, someone having T-shirts made wants to see the conditions for workers are good. Or you are supplied food products and want to see where it grows and the facilities where it's produced and packaged. These conditions can never be properly assessed through a flat screen.

- Location. Your company may have offices in various locations and it's helpful to visit so you know the environment. Or you may need to inspect something for work purposes, such as a plot of land you're interested in.

- Attending meetings and events. You need to attend a meeting, lecture, exhibition or show that's relevant to your business.

- Search the world. You want to look for or confirm new products are right for your business. You want to meet potential new suppliers or employees.

- Doing a deal. Business advisers Oxford Economics discovered through research that potential customers are nearly twice as likely to sign with you if you have a face-to-face meeting. So it's definitely worth making that trip to see them.

- Incentives. These trips are to motivate employees, and involve such as going on team-building weekends – which although might involve a leisure event are essentially for business purposes.

Business travel in some form has been undertaken since the time people started trading with each other. In fact, many of today's roads started as thoroughfares for people taking such as livestock or their wares to a weekly market.

In the 1800s, the advent of trains further increased business travel. Then it started literally taking off in the 1960s with the arrival of reasonably priced and plentiful flights.

So we should remember that today's business travellers are in a line from the innovators of centuries gone by – and without them, we might never have tasted such delights as tea, coffee and even chocolate.

How to Travel in Business Class

Flying business class is a whole new world. A world of lounges, leg room, proper champagne, celebrity chef-prepared meals and sleep – actual, full body reclined sleep.

But before you get too excited, there are a few things to know about flying business class that can make already very pleasurable experience even more glamorous.

1. Check-In

When checking in at the airline counter, international business class customers are often granted 'express entry' cards for customs, making the check-in to business lounge time a smooth transition.

2. The Business Lounge

Be sure to arrive early enough to enjoy the lounge amenities. Depending on the airline you're flying with, check who that airline partners with internationally to find out which lounge you will have access to, for example, if you're flying Qantas business, you'll have access to the Emirates business lounge in Dubai. And even if you're flying a smaller airline, say Philippines Airlines from Brisbane, you'll have access to the Qantas lounge.

Sure your business class boarding pass gets you entry into the business lounge, your dress code is what seals the deal between you and bottomless sparkling wine, petit fours and cheese platters.

3. What to wear in Business Class

The general rule of thumb when it comes to the business class dress code for most is smart casual, so you can still get away with your comfy flying pants however thongs (flip-flops), beachwear or clothing with offensive images or slogans are not permitted. So if you were tossing up wearing your fav Tupac shirt with the marijuana leaves all over it, maybe err on the side of caution and don't.

4. Business Class Etiquette

Once you're in the lounge act cool, but totally help yourself to a couple of pre-flight mimosas, a quick stack of pancakes and barista-made coffee. Remember though, you want to stay hydrated and sober for your flight, so keep it classy and limit your intake of free drinks, because guess what? There's more coming.

5. Drinks on Arrival

Remember economy flights? The humiliation of having to walk through business class and seeing those bubbling champagne flutes pass you by, as you kept trudging your way to the back of the plane mouth parched? Well, those flutes are now yours. Sit down, relax and get ready to be waited on hand and foot.

6. Hungry?

Business Class serves an entree, main and dessert along with plenty of moreish snacks. The best part? Say goodbye to plastic cutlery; business class is silver service all the way.

7. Still Thirsty?

Be careful the bubbles and cocktails don't go to your head. We know, it's gotten bigger since flying business, but you don't want the hosts to judge you. They'll happily refill your glass, but aim to keep your blood alcohol at the kind of level where you're sufficiently buzzed enough to enjoy the ride, but not enough that you start telling the person next to you your deepest darkest secrets. A Bloody Mary is always a good option when you'd like another beverage but are trying to appear to be 'healthy'.

How to get Discounts on a Business Class Ticket

First Class and Business Class air travel is expensive and can run to thousands of dollars for an international round trip. Here are a few tips to help you cut the cost of flying in the premium cabins.

Steps

1. Be flexible with your actual travel dates and book in advance to get the cheaper fares. Many online booking engines such as Orbitz and Travelocity have flexible date search tools which are very helpful in tracking down the lowest available airfare over a set period of time. Always select "lowest fare" when doing an airfare search online.

2. Never book too close to your departure day as you will probably then have to pay the full published fare which can be very expensive. First class full fare tickets are generally only bought by corporate travellers on business.

3. Avoid peak business travel days like Monday and Friday. Add a Saturday night stay to reduce the fare further.

4. Experiment with your departure airport for your trip – this may sometimes throw out a lower fare. Many online booking engines such as Orbitz will allow you to check prices from nearby airports.

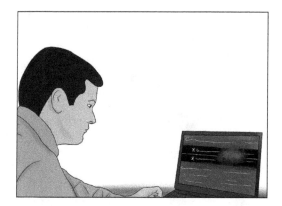

5. Consider ground transportation costs, especially if your departure airport is some distance away. If you fly Virgin Atlantic Upper Class on a higher fare you will get complimentary chauffeur driven cars at both ends. For example, passengers to Los Angeles can be driven to any desired location in California.

6. Flying through a hub connection airport is often cheaper than flying non-stop - but does any saving justify the extra inconvenience? Good deals can also be found booking overnight 'red-eye' flights - those comfortable first class seats will help you sleep better.

7. Check the price of your flight online with a number of major booking engines to ensure you cover all the GDS's (Global Distribution Systems) - these are the 4 mainframe databases which power the airfare market worldwide - Sabre, Worldspan, Galileo and Amadeus. Some online agents are

biased towards a single GDS so you will want to cover all your bases by checking elsewhere. Then double check any prices found directly at the airline websites.

8. With codeshare flights (for example, Lufthansa and USAir, be aware that the same flight may be priced differently on the sites of the codesharing airlines.

9. Phone your travel agent to see if they can beat your online quote. Also use a specialist business class / first class consolidator who will have access to many unpublished airfares not available elsewhere. Generally, using a consolidator is optimal when booking around 4 to 8 weeks in advance.

How to Behave when Flying First Class

Flying first class is an opportunity very few people get to experience. Flying in luxury is not just about unlimited champagne and comfy seats, but it's rather about your entire deportment and conduct from the minute you set foot into the airport facility all the way through to arriving to your destination. Whether you are a first time first class passenger trying not to be over awed or a seasoned veteran of premier travel attempting to avoid the contempt of familiarity, start at step one to find out how you should act on your next journey in First Class.

Part 1. First Class Lounge

1. Mingle with people. The first class lounge is your first destination after the security check-point. It is a place where you can socialize with other people and share the destination you are going, and listen to others. You may be in the presence of high powered executives or even various celebrities.

- There have been many stories where people have flown first class and have been befriended by a celebrity and invited to an upcoming party or VIP event.

- The first class lounge is known to be rather quiet due to not many people flying in luxury.

2. Be polite to your host or concierge. You will most likely be assigned a host or concierge when you check into the lounge. These people are highly trained and equipped with well-esteemed communicating and facilitating skills. They will be able to help you each step of the way from checking in to boarding. Be courteous and respectful and avoid being too demanding when requesting various things.

- It's seen to be a great quality if you are able to remember your concierge or host's name. They will remember yours, so show them your erudition by recalling theirs. There is a host or concierge in the luxury lounge and then a few while on the flight. Don't be to offended if you don't click with your initial attendant; however it is highly unlikely that you won't be taken aback with the service they want to lavish on you.

Part 2. First Class Boarding

1. Be punctual. It's important to be as poised as you can at all times. Show that you can be well-revered by practicing punctuality upon arrival and also when it's time to board. Understand that it will be relaxed in the luxury lounge, and your host or concierge will remind you prior to being escorted to your seat on the flight.

- Avoid doing thing's like showering or ordering big meals only prior to boarding. If you have a big stop-over or waiting time, you may have adequate time to do these things. Fend to be ready to go at least 30-45 minutes before the expected boarding time.

- Understand that holding up people when boarding is actually holding up the entire airline from Economy to First Class. Because you will be the first group boarding and settling in, it's important to show respect by being where you need to be at the right time so thing's run smoothly and you can get to your destination on-time.

2. Exercise humility. There is no need to rush, you have a verified seat on the plane, so show humility by letting other first class passengers board or seat before you. This is a sign of respect and implies that you are a person with a dignified nature.

3. Thank your first class host. Before you depart on the next leg of your journey, it's important to say farewell and thank your host from the first class lounge, you may never see them again. If you feel so inclined, you could tip them for their service as a sign of your appreciation before they hand you over to your next porter.

Part 3. In-Flight

1. Be very kind to your in-flight attendants. The flight hosts that will be serving you during the flight are hospitality veterans and seasoned professionals, not just flight attendants. Be very kind to these people and use your manners extensively. They will be doing everything they can for you, and it's simple protocol to treat them with reverence.

2. Try to acquaint yourself with others. It's most likely that you will be seated next to someone in

most aircraft's. Although, you will have your own room and space to enjoy the flight, it's very respectful and kind of you to introduce yourself to people within reach. This could lead to some very interesting conversation that will will make time fly.

- You can learn a lot from others, even more so the people that fly in first class due to their presumed success.

3. Smile graciously. Show that you are having a good time by smiling at service attendants and other passengers while you reside in the first class area. It's evident that most people in First Class will be very friendly and excited due to the relaxed environment.

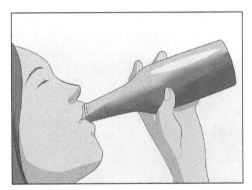

4. Go easy on the alcohol. In most flights there is a private first class bar with a broad range of beverages. You will most likely have your own small range of alcohol in your little luxury pod; however it's important to stay modest and avoid getting sloshed. You want to be able to remember the experience and not ruin it by getting ridiculously intoxicated.

5. Be mindful and respectful of others. Some people are rather reclusive and don't wish to mingle

more than they have to. It's esteemed that you honor other peoples desires by not forcing them or pushing them to interact with you. If however you are a reclusive person and don't wish to mingle, respect others that want to. Be polite if you're introduced to someone, however it's fine if you tell someone that you would rather be left to your own devices.

6. Tread lightly in conversation. When talking with any strangers or new friends, it's important to tread lightly in conversation and avoid topics that require responses on political stances and things of that nature. Keep questions light as you get to know other people; you might ask why they are flying, and where they are visiting.

Part 4. Acting around Celebrities and Executives

1. Be down-to-earth. It's very evident that you may be acquainted with a familiar face while you fly in complete luxury. When you meet the icon or are given the opportunity to speak with them, treat them like they were just another person. This is usually the way they wish to be treated.

- By being down-to-earth and relaxed, you're on the same level as the other person and the atmosphere is far from elated.

- Be you and be normal. Don't request the person to sing if they are a singer, or request any other strange activities for you to be able to remember. Understand that even though you might be on vacation, they are more than likely at work.

2. Let them lead the conversation. The individual you meet and speak with have spoken to numerous people in their success. Just let them ask the questions and lead the conversation. If you have questions to ask them, be sure to keep them to a modest number and avoid plucking at topics and questions that are personal or not of your concern.

3. Be polite when requesting an autograph. Understand that the personage is probably tired, nervous or wanting a nice and laid back flight to their next destination. If you're the irritating fan or follower wanting them to sign every last item that you are carrying, you will come across as a goose and probably be removed from seeing the celebrity by in-flight security.

• Fend to only request one autograph signing and if given the opportunity, one qualitative photo.

• Refrain from asking the person to add or follow you on social networking if you do not know them personally or aren't at the same 'status' as them. If you are an executive or figure yourself, ask your publicist (if you have one) to go and ask theirs if you can sojourn with them for a while.

Part 5. Dining

1. Order food appropriately. First class flying has plenty of perks and one of them would be the opportunity to enjoy gourmet food over 35,000 feet (10,668.0 m) in the air. Aim to order what you know when it comes to dining though. There would be nothing worse than realizing that you are allergic to a certain ingredient while you want to experience first class flying in the best state you can.

- Because the flight only has a trained nurse on-board, if something does unfortunately go wrong in relation to food, you may not have all the medical assistance you will require.

- It's fine to save the opportunity to enjoy a delectable seafood dish at your hotel or restaurant on land. You could aim to eat things like salads, sandwiches, soups or a banquet of finger food to share with the Lady or Gentleman next to you if you feel so inclined.

2. Voice your special requirements. If there is something an airline knows what to do extensively, that would be food variety. Even economy has a few options in their section, but because you are in first class, take the opportunity to suit the food to your pallet or requirement(s). Remember to ask your concierge or flight host to check with recipes that they meet your dietary needs.

- If you have allergies like an allergy to nut products, be sure to ask a host to see the in-flight chef if they can cook a dish that usually requires a nut ingredient, to be substituted. The chefs on-board are professionally picked, and it's their job to meet the demands of first class passengers.

3. Personally compliment the chef. After you have treated your taste buds to some of the globes most gourmet dishes, it's a great idea to go and compliment the Chef face-to-face. This meek gesture will be well-revered by others around you, and you may even get a complimentary dessert or get to taste one of their new decadent creations.

- Chefs in First Class are usually very friendly and laid back individuals who like a good gastronomic chat. If you know a thing or two about the culinary arena, or perhaps want to learn more, it's encouraged after the dining service, to meet and converse with the chef(s).

Part 6. Concluding your Journey

1. Show appreciation. At the end of your voyage you should strive to thank everyone who made your experience worth-while. Thank your flight host or concierge by name and wish them an enjoyable rest of their day. It's even more encouraged to let the flight hosts know what you really admired during the flight.

- A gratified individual is highly revered and you will be remembered if in the unlikely case you get the same host or concierge on your journey home.

- In some flights you are able to meet the pilot. It's encouraged to warmly shake his or her hand and thank them sincerely for such an enjoyable flight. You will make their day to know that what they love doing is ultimately bringing the world closer together.

2. Take all belongings. Remember to not leave anything behind except your smile and polite demeanor. Prior to landing and then again before exiting the aircraft, double-check under seats, arm rests etc. for any personal items that may be mislaid.

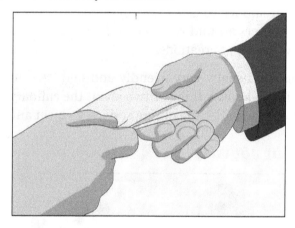

3. Try donating to the charity. It's most likely that the flight will have donation slips for a charity that they sponsor. If you don't have one in your arm-rest or seat pocket, you can ask for a spare one from your flight host. It's a sweet gesture and it will certainly not go unobserved.

4. Write a review. You can express your appreciation by visiting the airlines website or airline review websites and write about your experience to inspire others to fly First Class and provide insight for the carriers probable candidates.

How to Book a Hotel Room

Finding a good hotel and making a reservation can be stressful, especially if you are trying to book a hotel room for a large family or at the last minute. With many hotel reservations done online, there are online tools you can use to compare rates and shop around before booking the right room for you and your family. If you have never booked a hotel room before, you can do so easily and quickly by following several simple steps.

Part 1. Finding a Good Hotel

1. Determine your budget. Before you look for a hotel and make a reservation, you want to ensure the hotel will meet your budget and your needs. You should first determine your budget, or how much you can spend, when booking a hotel room. This will help you narrow down your search and be efficient with the time you spend looking for a hotel and booking a room.

   • Having a limited budget does not mean you will end up staying in a cheap, dirty hotel. In fact, there are many discount options available for visitors on a budget.

   • On the flip side, you may be travelling for work and have the ability to expense your accommodations to your company's account. In this case, an affordable hotel rate may not be as much of a priority for you.

2. Think about your required accommodations during your stay. Do you require enough room for a family of four, or do you just need enough room for yourself? Consider how big you would like the hotel room to be, including how many beds you require and how many bathrooms. If you are

traveling with your family, you may need two queen beds and one large bathroom. If you are traveling solo, you may just need one queen bed and one decently sized bathroom.

- If you require disability facilities, call the hotel to confirm if they are wheelchair accessible or offer disability amenities.

- Consider whether or not you require extra amenities, such as a spa or a fitness center. If you need a solid internet connection, look at hotels that offer free Wi-Fi as part of the nightly rate.

- If you are traveling as a family or in a big group, you might want to consider booking a suite with separate living area and bedroom so that the whole group can be accommodated without space and privacy constraints.

3. Identify your ideal location or area. Sometimes, location can trump budget or required accommodations, especially if you are look for a location that is convenient. Are you looking for a hotel that is close to a work event or conference? Are you looking for a hotel that is close to a specific tourist attraction? You may decide to stay in a location that is central or downtown, which will allow you to access different parts of the city easily. Or, you may decide to choose a more secluded location so you have some privacy and can drive or walk to and from the main areas of town.

- If you are traveling for business, you may decide to search for hotels that are close to a work conference or meeting.

- If you are traveling for pleasure, look for hotels that are walking distance to a hot spot, or hotels that offer packages that include car rentals so that you can get around easily.

4. Search for hotels online. The quickest way to look for hotels is online through a hotel search

engine. These search engines will allow you to specify your planned days of travel, how many nights you require, your ideal location, and your required amenities, if any. You can also specify how much you are willing to spend on the hotel.

- Once you enter this information into the search engine, you will be presented with several hotel options. You can order the options from lowest to highest in terms of price, or use the map option to look at hotels that are closer to a certain area or location.

- Keep in mind that online search engines don't always show extra surcharges or fees for rooms. Note any small print next to the price for the room before you consider it.

- Some credit cards and AAA providers offer hotel search services and discounts to their members. Contact your credit card company or AAA provider for more information.

5. Compare hotels using discounted search tools. You can also use discounted search tools to compare several hotel options at once. All you need to do is specify your travel dates and your price points. These online sites will then search multiple databases for you and present several hotel options that best match your needs and that are discounted or offer cheaper rates.

- Read the reviews for the hotels you are considering to get a sense of cleanliness, customer service, and amenities. Weigh the reviews against the price and location of the hotel to determine if it will meet your needs.

- Some discounted search tools require you to book the hotel room before knowing exactly which hotel you were be staying in. Always read the fine print before you book a room to ensure you're not surprised by any restrictions or stipulations.

6. Call the hotel to get a better rate. Calling the hotel directly can land you a last minute booking or

a better rate. You may also be able to get a better sense of the customer service offered at the hotel, as you will be able to speak to the front desk and ask them specific questions about the hotel. Try to call in the late evening, as the mornings and afternoons are often busy for the front desk. You may want to ask questions such as:

- Is there a restaurant or bar on site? Is breakfast included in the nightly rate?

- Do you offer non-smoking rooms?

- Is the hotel near public transportation? Do you offer transportation like rental bikes?

- How far is the hotel from a specific location or area, such as the beach?

- Which side of the hotel has a better view or less noise?

- Is the area around the hotel safe?

- Are there facilities available for the disabled?

- What is the hotel's cancellation policy?

Part 2. Booking the Hotel

1. Reserve the room online. Once you have selected your hotel room, you can reserve it online through the hotel website. You will need to provide basic information about yourself for the booking, such as your full name and your travel dates.

- You can also reserve the room by calling the hotel directly. Try to call late evening as mornings and mid afternoons can be busy for the front desk.

- If you are looking for a group rate for a conference or a wedding, call the hotel directly and speak to the front desk. Many hotels do not advertise group rates online and can often offer you better rates over the phone.

2. Pay for the room with your credit card. Many online bookings will require payment via a credit card. If you are traveling on a business trip, you may use the company credit card to pay for the hotel.

- Always check if your credit card or AAA provider offers any discounts on hotels so that you can use them when you pay for the room.

- If you are staying at the hotel for an extended period of time, you may be able to pay for the first 2 to 3 nights upfront and then cover the rest of your stay once you get to the hotel. You will then be required to leave your credit card number on file and settle your bill at the front desk on your check out day.

3. Confirm the room is booked. You can confirm the hotel room is reserved by printing out a receipt at the end of your online booking session. You can also ask the hotel to send you a receipt as proof of payment if you book the hotel over the phone.

4. Read over your receipt to confirm that everything is correct. This includes your travel dates and agreed-upon room rates. The hotel should specify all regulatory fees and charges before you pay for the room or reserve the room. Extra fees, such as a cleaning fee or a parking fee, should be explained to you by the hotel so you are not surprised by any hidden fees when you check out.

How to Prepare for an Important Meeting Abroad

If you are planning to travel overseas, here's how you can prepare for a corporate meeting abroad.

Create an Itinerary

There's nothing like a face-to-face meeting with a client or customer. But, even the most minor mistakes can cost you valuable time and money you probably don't want to waste. Luckily, creating a well-planned itinerary will help ensure corporate meetings abroad run as smoothly as possible. Unique business ideas are great but presentation is equally important. In order to prepare accordingly, business men and women should think about what they aim to achieve, and their agenda priorities. Generally, it is better to have two to three appointments (or meetings) confirmed up to two months in advance, ensuring they are spaced comfortably throughout the day or time spent abroad, allowing a buffer for any unexpected occurrences.

Find Information on the Culture

Before you travel, invest some time in learning about the history and culture of the country you are visiting by attending cross-cultural seminars, or if this isn't possible, a search on the web can still be effective. Ensure you are aware of the differences in negotiating styles and attitudes towards punctuality, as well as understand the use of names and title. While the Japanese consider it rude to be late for a business meeting, in Latin countries, being late for a business meeting is more acceptable.

Check Travel Advisories

Before you even plan a corporate meeting abroad, check travel advisories. Governments across the world issue advisories regarding safety concerns that may affect travel to and from a particular region or country. They are released for a series of reasons, including the threat of terrorism, likelihood of natural disasters, political unrest, risk of war and health-related emergencies. However, these advisories don't always apply to the entire country, so before you travel, check to find out exactly where the advisory applies.

Plan Ahead to Stay Connected Abroad

Successful preparation for corporate meetings abroad could be as simple as making guests aware that a plug or adapter may be needed to charge laptops and mobile phones abroad. While this may seem obvious to some, others get caught up at work and completely forget.

To find out about additional international options for business trip, contact your cell phone provider. You may be able to sign-up to a temporary mobile phone plan for the duration of your visit to another country, to ensure you are able to make international phone calls abroad with ease.

Get a Visa

Depending on where you're corporate meeting is commencing, some foreign countries require business men and women to apply for a visa before they travel. However, the rules for each country vary significantly. The best method to prepare in advance involves calling the consulate for the country you are traveling to. More often than not, you will be asked to apply for the visa in person – and not online. To avoid wasting time, ensure you've prepared all the relevant documents.

Travel Budgeting and Finances

Planning a travel budget and calculating the finance required for a tour or vacation is vital to traveling. Expenses may vary greatly depending on the form of transportation, accommodation or food one opts for. Further, sightseeing tours, museum fees, recreational activity prices, etc. also need to be considered while planning a travel budget. The topics elaborated in this chapter on traveling on a limited budget, exchanging currency and getting the best exchange rates in a country, using travel vouchers, finding travel discounts, etc. are aimed at providing innovative insights into travel budgeting and finances.

How to Travel on a Very Limited Budget

Totally broke and dying to get out of town? Looking for some adventure without breaking the bank? This topic will explore some ideas for how you can travel as cost-effectively as possible, perhaps even for free. The key is do some research and be flexible.

Steps

1. Choose a mode of travel that fits within your budget and which you are comfortable with. Here are your options, from the cheapest to the most expensive:

- Hitchhiking. It's generally safe if you do it during the day, and seasoned hitchhikers can cross the entire US in four days or less.

- Train hopping. It's free, but it can also be dangerous and stressful. Looking over your shoulder for train yard workers and being ready to hop out of a moving vehicle when someone gets creepy with you may not be everyone's idea of fun. In addition, this is illegal, and may net you felony trespassing charges if you are caught.

- Canoe. If you have one and the weather is good, consider canoe camping.

- Take a bicycle ride. You don't move as far as a car in one day, but you cover more territory than walking. Like hiking, you get to see the countryside up close and meet interesting people. Bicycle Touring.

- Motorcycle or scooter. If you have one already, it's just about the cheapest way to propel yourself over long distances, because of the low fuel costs. If you don't have one, look into the cost of renting and compare it to the next few options.

- Buses and trains. This is safer than the previous options, but you'll need to check the fares for the trip you have in mind to determine how cost-effective it is.

- Driving. This is comparable to bus and train fares in terms of gas costs, but if you don't have a car, you'll have to rent one, which can get pretty pricey. However, there are several ways to push down the cost of driving:

- Carpool and split the gas/rental costs. If your friends don't want to come along, check the rideshare section of your local craigslist:

- Sleep in your car. This will save you money on lodging, unless you were going to secure free lodging anyway.

- Hypermile. If you follow the techniques carefully, you can save plenty of money on gas.

2. Plan where you will sleep.

- Sleep on the couch. Even if you don't have friends you can stay with, there are a few ways to get around that:

- Network. Ask everyone you know or even anyone you chat with throughout the day if they know of anyone you can stay with. Ask in your Twitter, Myspace, and Facebook updates.

- House-sitting is a good method of obtaining free shelter, though it comes with responsibilities. Some websites list house-sitting opportunities for free, and others will charge you.

- If you live in a city or region where others want to travel, you can arrange a temporary home-swap with people who live wherever you'd like to stay. This can be coordinated through Craigslist and other sites.

- Sleep in your car. Many interstate rest areas allow overnight parking. Vans, pick-up trucks with camper tops, and even small hatchbacks with the rear seat folded down can make comfy beds. And you will be especially thankful when the rain starts pouring down, and you can just pull over and not worry about setting up a tent.

- Go camping. In state and national parks in the US, campsites are often cheap, or even free. (Chain campsites, and large resort-type ones with pools and arcades will often cost you as much as a hotel would.)

- Look for hostels. This dorm-style lodging is usually cheaper than motels.

3. Plan how you will eat. Generally, the less prepared food you buy, the better.

- If you have or can borrow a camp stove, you would be surprised how easy it is to cook a cheap and delicious pasta feast in a parking lot or rest stop.

- Stuff a jar of peanut butter and some crackers in your pack to save you from the overpriced gas station snacks.

- Dumpster Dive. This can also be useful for finding cans and glass bottles and getting cash for them in some cases.

- Find Wild Edible Plants - especially berries (like dewberries) and other fruit. If you're in the desert, you might be able to gain sustenance from yucca and prickly pear cactus. A word of caution, however, be sure you know what you are eating and that it is edible. Some berries and other plants are very similar to others that are very lethal. As long as you know what you're eating berries and other plants are a great way to get free food.

- Bring energy bars. They might be expensive, but they'll hold you over when you need to avoid the temptation of buying food at a restaurant so you can wait until you get to a grocery store and buy much cheaper food that you can cook yourself. If you have the time, you can make your own energy bars before you go.

4. Brainstorm ways to make money on the road, if you need to.

- Can you play an instrument? An afternoon of busking on a busy city street may get you some cash to buy a meal or gas to get you to your next destination.

- Panhandle Please note that panhandling is illegal in some places. Know the law to keep yourself from getting in trouble.

- Farm labor. Go to websites that list farms and farm work opportunities and look for operations in the areas you plan to travel through. Call in advance and ask if you can work for a full day. If they can't give you cash, maybe they'll give you food and/or lodging.

- Two good farm listing sites in the US are Local Harvest and ATTRA.

5. Bring helpful tools and supplies.

- A comfortable bag. You might need to do a lot of walking, so choose a backpack intended for that purpose. Make sure it has support straps across your hips and shoulders, and the straps should be padded.

- A folding bike. If you're not traveling with your own means of transportation, a portable bike could be a sensible investment for if you need to travel from your campsite or the place you're staying to a local grocery store, or so you can explore areas easily when you're not hitchhiking. When you're not using it, you can fold the bike and carry it with you.

- Baby wipes. Bathing can become an issue when traveling in this fashion. You may not have daily and immediate access to a suitable shower. Baby wipes will allow you to freshen up easily. You can buy some or, better yet, make your own.

- Camp stove. As mentioned earlier, this is handy for making your own food anywhere.

6. Scour freebie websites before you leave.

- Most major cities have all types of free entertainment and services; which can be found, on sites like Lafreebeee and Freecycle.org, depending on where you live.

- Museums are free on certain days of the month or if you have a student id.

- You can see free movie screenings if you know where to look and how to sign up.

- Sign up for free coupon offers and take the coupons with you on your trip.

- There are free medical clinics in many major cities.

- Free food coupons can be found on Fatwallet.com and Freestufftimes.

How to Calculate Cost of Travel

Any time you plan a trip, it is helpful to know how much it will cost to travel to and from your destination. Several factors must be taken into consideration in order to get an accurate figure for the amount of money a trip will cost. Follow these steps to calculate cost of travel.

Steps

1. Calculate the cost of transportation. Transportation is likely to be 1 of the biggest travel costs you will incur. If you are taking a plane, train or bus, then your transportation cost equates to the price of your ticket. If you are driving, you will need to calculate the cost of the rental vehicle, if applicable, and the amount of gas your trip will require. This is mostly aimed at cost per US or CAN Dollar, for UK Pound / Euro Dollar you may have to adjust manually.

   • Start with the distance you will be driving, in miles or kilometers.

   • Divide the distance by your car's fuel economy (miles per gallon or kilometers per liter). The resulting amount is the number of gallons or liters it will take you to complete your trip.

   • Multiply the number of gallons or liters by the average cost of fuel.

   • Note: If you drive a rental vehicle, the rental company will charge you a fixed amount per mile and, additionally, a fixed amount for car insurance. Be sure to factor these amounts into your travel costs.

```
Food = $200
Lodging = $1000
Tolls = $50
Parking = $50
Depreciation = $100
```

2. Include all costs that are incurred while traveling.

- Food and drink - If you travel for an extended period of time, you will need to stop for food and drink, or you may opt to pack food and drink. Either way, you must include this expense in your cost of travel calculation.

- Lodging - For trips that require driving for more than 1 day, you will need to stop over somewhere to get some sleep. Unless you opt to pull to the side of the road and sleep in your vehicle, you will need to add the cost of lodging to your overall travel costs.

- Tolls - Many road routes have a series of toll booths that you must stop at as you travel. The cost of tolls can add up, especially if you are on a long road trip.

- Parking - If you opt to take a plane, train or bus, then you may need to add the cost of storing your automobile in a parking lot or garage to your travel costs.

- Depreciation - Any time you drive your vehicle, the value of your vehicle depreciates, and that figure must be added to your cost of travel calculation. Depreciation can be figured by multiplying the average cost of depreciation, 27 cents per 1 mile (5 cents per 1.6 km), by the distance you will be traveling.

- Indirect costs - Indirect travel costs should be considered if you are driving, and include things like road maintenance, pollution, government taxes, accidents and land use. To calculate indirect costs, multiply .05 cents by the number of miles or .01 cents by the number of kilometers you will be driving.

- Time to travel - Also consider your time on the road vs. destination if you're going on vacation; to calculate this take the hours it will take to travel to your destination, add each stop point time (food, restroom, refuel) per 15min increments, and you will have a total time to get to your destination. If you want to figure out how much 'money' you have lost in your delays (an average time vs. pay for your job if you're traveling for such a reason) take the amount you're getting paid total to arrive on time and subtract 10 cents for every 5 min you are not traveling, this will give you an average cost of what you will lose or gain for being on time.

3. If you have to, consider time taken off work. When figuring the cost to travel, the time you miss from work must be added to the equation. Take the number of hours you will be missing and multiply that by the amount of money you make per hour.

How to Exchange Currency

Many international travelers exchange currency before they depart, so they have at least a little money for a cab at the airport or other immediate expenses. Once you reach your destination, you are likely to find currency exchange kiosks at airports, ferry terminals, hotels and other areas where tourists congregate. However, these tend to charge more than banks – total fees sometimes run upwards of 7 percent. There are other ways to save, however, if you're willing to plan ahead a little.

Part 1. Exchanging Currency at Home

1. Understand the process so that you get the best deal. If you've never exchanged currency before, it's a good idea for you to understand a bit about the process so that you don't get any expensive surprises. The general idea is that you'll find a business that exchanges currency, and they'll give you the currency that you want in exchange for a small fee (plus, obviously, the amount of money you want changed). Now, in addition to this, it's important to understand that some currencies are worth more than others. For example, a single euro is usually equivalent to $1.30 USD or .80 GBP. How much the difference is will fluctuate, usually with the state of those economies. So, even though you're exchanging $100, you may only get out 75 euro.

- Your goal, then, is to exchange currency when your currency is high and the foreign currency is low, because this means that you'll get more of the foreign money than you would otherwise.

- Understand that the dollar (for example) being worth less than the euro doesn't have much to do with the cost of items. The relative cost of items is determined by the market in that area. So, for example, a banana in the US is much cheaper than a banana in Sweden, even though the dollar is strong compared to krona.

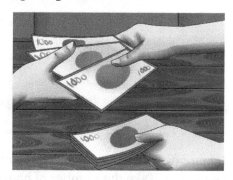

2. Do exchange some money before you leave. The ideal ratio told by multiple Pro travelers is 80:20

(the famous Pareto principle). Buy 20% in cash and 80% in Forex card. It is important to exchange some money before you leave for your trip. You'll probably encounter the advice that it's better to exchange currency in the country you're traveling to and that's usually true if you are exploring common countries. However, if it's a relatively off the chart country, then you may not want to follow this advice. To understand this, you must know that there are two kinds of currencies; one is those who get highly traded, Like Euro, USD, etc. The other is less traded ones, also known as Exotic currencies. It's always better to buy Exotic currency at the location but exchanging it with USD (because USD is the global currency). However, you will want to have some cash prepared for when you arrive. There is going to be some amount of travel time, between landing in your destination and getting the chance to exchange more money, where lots of things can go wrong. It's a good idea to have a little cash on hand, including small bills and coins if possible, so that you're prepared for anything.

- The amount that you should have will vary by where you're traveling to, but the equivalent of $40 USD is generally a good starting point, if you're going to be in your destination for more than 3 days.

3. Look at the status of the exchange rate. Before you exchange money or decide how much to exchange, do a little research on the exchange rate. The rate will fluctuate and if you're likely to exchange a lot of money, you'll want to time it carefully so that you don't lose too much money. Generally, you're better off waiting to exchange most of your money until you arrive. However, if the rate for your home currency is falling, you're better off exchanging almost everything you'll need before you go.

- Googling "currency exchange rate" will bring up a chart for your chosen currencies, letting you gauge where your currency currently sits.

4. Go to your bank. The easiest place to exchange currency when you're at home is at your bank.

Go to the banking institution that you use and tell them that you'd like to exchange currency. The upside of bank exchanging is that most banks will charge only a very small fee for exchanging currency (if they charge a fee at all) and you'll know you're getting a good rate.

- The only trick here is that, unless it is a very major bank in a very major city, they're unlikely to have the currency on hand. You'll need to order the currency at least a few days and sometimes as much as two weeks in advance. Plan ahead.

5. Get a traveler-friendly account. Before you leave, call your bank or go in and ask about what their policy is of charging your card overseas. Many banks will charge you a fee for using your card, at an ATM, foreign bank, for writing checks, etc. when you're overseas. If they charge a lot of fees, you might want to see about starting up a separate bank account with another bank. Shop around until you find a bank that charges low or no fees at all. Then, transfer your money into that account. You can then use this account whenever you want to travel abroad.

- Some banks charge a monthly fee for having below a certain amount of money in your account. If you plan on keeping a traveler's account, you'll want to plan on keeping at least a certain amount of money in the account at all times, to avoid incurring fees.

6. Buy cash online. It is possible to order money online as well. This will need to be done before you leave, as it isn't particularly safe to do once you arrive. The rates tends to be up-to-date and the fees fair, but the cost to have the money shipped to you can make this option undesirable. If you're feeling a bit lazy, however, this can save you a trip to the bank.

- The best time to do this is if you're planning on getting a lot of cash exchanged. If you order a large amount, somewhere in the hundreds to thousands of dollars, then you can ask them to waive the delivery fees. Some companies may do this and it makes the rate you get much more reasonable.

Part 2. Exchanging Currency Abroad

1. Be prepared to pay cash. When you travel outside of your country, you should be prepared to pay cash for a lot more services and products that you normally would at home. Not all countries have the widespread use of cards that is seen in English speaking countries. This means that you should be aware that you might have to pay for things with cash that you're accustomed to using your card to buy normally. Plan ahead.

- This is especially common in poorer countries. They often have less infrastructure for the widespread use of cards.

2. Use an ATM. Your best bet for exchanging currency when you're traveling is to use an ATM. Find an ATM with a major bank in the area and then, so long as you have one of the major VISA or Master/Maestro cards, you'll be able to do basic transactions like withdrawing money. This will usually give you the best rate and if you have a travel-friendly bank, you'll hardly pay any fees at all.

- Finding an ATM can be tricky. Your best bet will be to let Google be your guide. Get to a place, early on, where you will have internet access and then ask Google Maps for the locations of all nearby ATMs. You can also usually locate an ATM by locating a bank. If you don't know where to find those, ask a local hotel concierge or taxi driver.

3. Pay with your card. When you can, simply pay for items and services with your card. As long as it's one of the major cards (VISA or Master/Maestro card), any business that takes credit and debit cards should be able to take your card without problems. This is handy because your bank will simply exchange the money on their end and you don't have to worry about exchanging currency yourself much at all.

- Be aware, however, that you may encounter problems with the card itself. Certain countries have switched to the more secure chip-and-pin system. Certain card readers will then be unable to read the traditional North American swipe card.

- Again, some banks charge extortionate fees for this. Know what your bank charges before you leave.

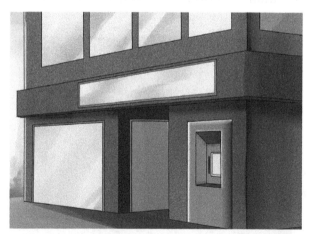

4. Go to a major local bank once you arrive. Just like you can exchange currency at home with a local bank, you can also use any bank once you arrive in your destination. This can be tricky but much like it is at home, you're more likely to get a legitimate rate and minimal fees.

- You might think the language barrier will be your biggest issue but as long as you're in a fairly large city and you go to a major bank in a central location, you're very likely to find at least one teller who speaks English.

- The main problem is that some banks won't exchange currency if you're not a customer. Your best bet is to ask around and hope for the best. If they won't exchange your currency, they'll probably at least be able to help you find a bank that will. They are much more likely to exchange your currency if you're withdrawing money using your card, since this is more secure for them.

- You can also ask your hotel concierge to help you find a bank that will exchange your currency.

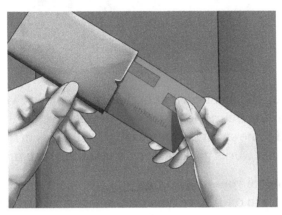

5. Buy a prepaid card. This is not your best option but it is an option that is available. Pre-paid cards are like debit cards but they have a set amount of cash on them. You can order these before you leave or you can buy them once you arrive. However, the rates on these tend to be terrible, some businesses may not accept them, and you're in hot water if you lose it. Still, for some people it might be the best option they have.

- Be extremely cautious when purchasing these cards. They should only come from reputable vendors.

Part 3. Getting the Best Rate

1. Plan ahead to prevent over-exchanging. Before you leave or at least before you exchange too much money, plan ahead on what you'll be doing and how much money you'll need. Exchange on the low side of how much you think you're going to use. This way, you won't risk over-exchanging and wasting money on having to exchange the money back once you return.

- This will also help you incur the minimum number of fees, if the exchange fee with your chosen method is a one-time fee (such as at an ATM or bank).

2. Do your research. Look up the most current exchange rate before you exchange money using a service, especially if you're using a currency exchange service specifically. Businesses that specialize in exchanging currency and some small businesses that exchange currency will both often give you an outdated exchange rate that works in their favor, so that they can make more money off of you.

- Download an app before you leave so that you can easily check the exchange rate on your phone. Just be careful to only leave data on when you're actively checking the rate, so that you don't go over on your data plan while you're abroad.

3. Shop around to get the best rate. Don't be afraid to find out what you can get at a different location. Banks may be less of an issue, although some banks might have less fees than others, but currency exchange businesses will definitely have very variable rates. This will also give you the added bonus of possibly being able to haggle with the business, since a small currency exchange will be more willing to fight for your business.

4. Pay in your own currency when you can. If you are in an area where you have the option to pay

in your own currency, do that. Usually, if a business allows this they will tell you or the price will be marked. Make sure you're informed about the exchange rate before paying, however. You can expect a small markup, so that they can pay the exchange fees on their end, but it should only be small.

- This is most common in areas and countries where your currency is very highly valued or is used frequently.

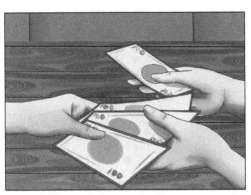

5. Exchange in the country you travel to. Most of the time, your best bet is to exchange your money in the country you travel to. This is especially true if you're coming from one of the major countries to a minor one, because your money will be more highly valued. The idea is that you want to carry as little cash on you as possible when you're traveling (although you can keep cash in hidden or secure locations, such as a hotel safe) so exchanging once you get there is better than possibly forgetting your wallet at an airport layover in Bangladesh.

6. Avoid the airport and hotels. Do not, as much as is humanly possible, exchange currency at an airport or hotel. You will get charged huge fees and you will get a terrible exchange rate. Be especially cautious if they advertise as having "zero fees" or "fee free", because those places will give you the worst exchange rate possible. Exchanging in either of these locations should be a last resort.

How to get the Best Exchange Rate when Traveling in a Foreign Country

Depending on where you travel, currency exchange rates can either help you get great bargains or make your trip surprisingly expensive. No matter how strong your home currency is relative to the local currency, however, you want to make sure you're getting the best exchange rate possible whenever you need to get cash or make a purchase.

Steps

1. Find out what your bank charges for foreign transactions. Most of the time, you'll get the best possible exchange rate when you use your credit or debit card, either to make purchases or to withdraw cash from an ATM. By doing so, you get the same exchange rates that the banks offer to each other, with no middleman adding extra fees for the exchange. Some banks and credit card companies, however, will charge you a fee of as much as 3 percent on foreign transactions, so you need to do some research before you leave home. Call your bank and ask them what they charge. If they charge a fee, call around and ask other banks what they're charging. You may be able to find a better deal, but you'll need to plan well ahead.

RATES TABLE

1.00 Euro Rates table

Top 10		Aug 12, 2013 04:05 UTC
Euro	**1.00 EUR**	**inv. 1.00 EUR**
US Dollar	1.332387	0.750532
British Pound	0.859933	1.162881
Indian Rupee	80.701265	0.012391
Australian Dollar	1.448016	0.690600
Canadian Dollar	1.370576	0.729620
Emirati Dirham	4.893796	0.204340
Swiss Franc	1.231193	0.812220
Chinese Yuan Renminbi	8.164651	0.122479
Malaysian Ringgit	4.317663	0.231607

2. Know the currency exchange rate. Before you set off for your trip, find out what the current exchange rate is. You can easily find this in many newspapers or online. Knowing the exchange rate is your most powerful defense against getting a bad deal, so find it out before you go, and periodically check on it while you're traveling. When you are abroad, don't just trust the signs at street kiosks. Verify the exchange rate online if at all possible.

3. Use your credit or debit card as much as possible. As mentioned, you're likely to get the best rate this way. Use your card for purchases as much as possible to avoid ATM fees. When you do use an ATM, be sure to check how much it will charge you--some foreign ATMs charge $5 or more. If the fee is more than a couple dollars, try to find another ATM.

4. Plan your budget while traveling. You don't want to carry a ton of cash with you, but you also should try to have enough cash so that you don't get stuck having to make a currency exchange at high rates. You're more likely to get a good rate in large cities than in small towns--in some countries, you won't even be able to exchange money outside the city.

5. Take out cash only as you need it, and try to plan your expenditures toward the end of your stay in any country. This will help you to minimize the risk of robbery or pickpockets and avoid getting stuck with excess cash when you leave.

6. Avoid the exchange companies and Cambio booths that you will see in most train stations and airports. They are convenient, and sometimes (especially in an emergency after banking hours) indispensable, but they frequently charge very high prices in return for the convenience. If you need to get cash, and you can't find an ATM, your best bet is to go to a large bank, post office or American Express office.

7. Haggle. While you won't be able to negotiate the rate at a bank, if you do get stuck changing money at a small vendor you may be able to haggle to get a better rate. It's critical to know the exchange rate before you do this, and sometimes it won't work, but it's worth a try, especially if there are many vendors in a small area.

8. Compare rates. It's especially important to shop around if you're using the exchange kiosks, but the rate you get can vary even from bank to bank. Try at least two or three different places before you settle on one.

Live Currency Rates	
Currency	**Rate**
EUR / USD	1.33237 ▲
USD / JPY	96.4807 ▼
GBP / USD	1.54948 ▼
USD / CHF	0.92415 ▲
USD / CAD	1.02883 ▼
EUR / JPY	128.547 ▼
AUD / USD	0.92021 ▲

9. Know the "real" rate. Sometimes the low rate posted will be the "sell" rate--you'll be charged the "buy" rate--or will only be applicable on very large or very small transactions. There may also be flat fees added to each transaction or extra commissions based on the amount of the exchange. You've got to watch out for these tricks and find out in advance the net amount you will receive from an exchange.

How to get and use the Travel Vouchers

With surges in fuel prices and baggage fees, paying for a flight can be very expensive. However, you do not always have to pay to fly. While nothing free comes easy, there are ways you can earn travel vouchers and frequent flyer miles that will get you free tickets.

Method 1. Receiving Travel Vouchers

1. Agree to be bumped. Major airlines tend to overbook their flights to compensate for passengers who may not show up. If more passengers show up than can fit on the airplane, the airline will ask for volunteers to take a different flight. To show their gratitude, they usually offer travel vouchers you can use on future flights. Just wait for an airline representative to announce that your flight has been overbooked, and then head to the counter to ask about being bumped.

- The voucher you receive will be used on your next trip, and the ticket you already purchased will be used on your current trip.

- If you do agree to be bumped for an offer, get the offer in writing. Ask the agent to write it down, sign it and maybe add their identification number. This will help you in case there is any question about your offer.

2. Volunteer to be bumped. As soon as you arrive to your flight terminal, go ahead and let the gate attendant know that you would be willing to be bumped if necessary. This way, instead of asking for volunteers, they can call your name if they end up needing to bump someone. Always be polite with the gate attendants so they are more willing to pick you to be bumped.

- Some airlines will ask you at baggage check if you are willing to be bumped, and others have an option at the electronic check-in where you can mark if you are willing to be bumped.

3. Get bumped by traveling at high peak times. Airports are busiest during Friday mornings and Sunday evenings or around holidays. Traveling when airlines tend to be overbooked will increase your chances of getting bumped and receiving airline vouchers.

- Try to fly to popular destinations and international airports. These flights are also likely to be overbooked. The more popular the airport, the more crowded the flights tend to be.

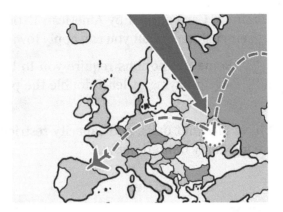

4. Book flights that have multiple stops. Flights that require you to connect to other flights before your final destination can help increase your chances of either missing a flight, having a cancelled flight, or getting bumped along the way. When this happens, you will most likely be offered a travel voucher.

- Pack lightly and avoid checking any bags. This way, if you get bumped to another flight, you will be ready to go. If you do check your bag to a different flight, you may have to wait a couple of days before you get your luggage.

5. Stay with one airline. It is easier to accumulate flying vouchers and frequent flyer miles if you keep using the same airline. By showing your loyalty, you may be eligible for extra perks and upgrades too.

6. Find companies that offer promotional vouchers. Some airline companies offer free or discounted vouchers for flight tickets. To find these deals, you need to look into airline benefits offered by different credit card companies on airline websites.

- The Delta SkyMiles Platinum Card offered by American Express offers a free companion voucher each year for their customers that you can apply toward a flight ticket.

- Watch out for bad deals. Some promotions require you to book through obscure travel agencies. Also, you may end up paying at least double the price of the ticket before you qualify for a "free" ticket.

- Watch for deals that have blackout dates and capacity restrictions. You may not want to pursue offers that have too many limitations.

Method 2. Earning Frequent Flyer Miles

1. Earn miles by using your credit card. If you choose a credit card that offers miles based on the money you spend, then you can end up flying for free. Once you have a travel rewards credit card with mileage rewards, use the card on all of your purchases. This is the fastest way to accumulate free miles. Just be sure to pay more than your minimum monthly payment each month or else your miles earned will be worth a fraction of the interest you will accumulate.

- For a typical rewards program, you may receive 1 mile (1.6 km) for every $1 spent.

- Delta offers a MileagePlus program that has been named the world's best frequent flyer program by Global Traveler magazine.

2. Apply for a credit card that offers a signing bonus. Some credit cards offer hundreds of thousands of frequent flyer miles just for choosing them. Do your due diligence, and shop around to find the best deals.

3. Earn flyer miles by shopping at online malls. Some airlines partner with certain popular department sores, home improvement stores, and other major online retailers where customers can earn extra miles when they make purchases. These malls can be found by checking on the airline's website. Here are several stores that have offered miles for purchases in the past:

- Crate and Barrel
- Best Buy
- The Container Store
- Sears
- Target
- Walmart

4. Get miles through airline promotions. When airlines are trying to gain more attention or beat out a competitor, they may offer extra miles to customers who fly certain flights. Usually, they will offer extra miles only for certain time blocks or destinations, but it is an easy way to accumulate flyer miles.

- Sing up for an airline's email list so you can be notified when they have promotional deals.

5. Watch for incentives offered by businesses. Many businesses are now trying to get your business by offering incentives like frequent flyer miles. Watch for deals offered by companies that you may want to take advantage of.

- For example, TD Ameritrade and Fidelity gave away frequent flyer miles for those who opened a non retirement brokerage account.

Method 3. Using Airline Connections

1. Work for an airline. Flight crews and most other airline employees receive free flight benefits. The perks range depending on the airline. Some airlines give two free flight tickets for their employees each year, and other airlines give discounted tickets that can be as much as a 90% reduction off the full ticket price.

- Southwest airline allows employees, spouses, eligible dependent children, and parents to fly on Southwest planes for free.

- American Airlines allow all of their employees to travel for free in coach class.

2. Find someone who works for an airline. Some airlines will offer their employees flight vouchers for family and friends. In recent years, airlines have tightened their policies on these types of vouchers, but they are still out there.

- Southwest Airlines has a guest pass program that gives unregistered friends and family members of employees a chance to fly for free.

- American Airlines has a program that allows employees to register family members who can then fly for free.

3. Fly standby. Some airline companies give their employees buddy passes to hand out to family and friends. However, the passes are only good as standby tickets. This means that you can only fly if there is an empty seat on the plane.

- Delta offers buddy passes to their employees.

- When using a buddy pass, you are seen as a representative of the airline. You are required to have a relaxed dress code, and maintain professional behavior.

- Be prepared for the flight you want to take to be full. You may have to wait for several flights before you find one that has room for you.

- It is best not to check any luggage when flying standby because you don't know which flight out you will take.

- Fly during slower times to increase your chances of making it on the plane.

How to Find Student Travel Discounts

Whether it is to visit family, go on vacation, or study abroad, traveling as a student can be expensive. Fortunately, there are many discounts and money-saving opportunities available just for students. To be a savvy student traveler, you should stay on top of the latest travel news and deals. Look around to see where you can save money on transportation and accommodations. You should also remember to bring your student ID with you as there are hundreds of student deals available at museums, theaters, special events, and more.

Method 1. Researching Good Deals

1. Use a student travel agency. Student travel agencies are online services that can help you connect to special deals and rates available only to students. These can offer rates that are not available anywhere else. They also sometimes offer special tours and group rates for students. You might try looking at:

- STA Travel

- Student Universe

- CheapOair

- Travelation

2. Read travel news. Travel websites and blogs can sometimes alert you when a special deal is available. When it comes to airfare and hotels, student discounts may be seasonal, so these websites can help you figure out when the best time to buy a ticket is. They can also offer tips for the student traveler on saving money.

- Travel newsletters, such as the ones offered by Travel Ticker or Travel Zoo, can sometimes inform you of special sales or temporary price reductions.

- The Student Travel Planning Guide offers advice and discounts to students traveling in groups.

- Go Abroad provides news, guides, and funding opportunities to students looking to study, volunteer, or teach abroad.

- Many news publications, such as US News and World Report or The Guardian, have travel sections that may post deals and discounts from time to time.

3. Apply for scholarships. Universities, foundations, charities, and even travel agencies sometimes offer special scholarships for students traveling abroad. While the scholarship may have special requirements that you must fulfill on the trip, these are a great way to find money to travel with. Some options include:

- Student Youth Travel Scholarships

- Rotary International Youth Exchange (for ages 15 to 19)

- uVolunteer Scholarship

4. Look up discounts for your specific destination. You may find that there are special discounts available to people traveling to your particular destination. You should also factor in when you are traveling, as you may find that there are more discounts during certain periods of the year.

- For example, if you are traveling to England in the spring, you can type into the search bar "student travel discounts England spring 2016."

- Try to determine when the tourism season is for your destination. During this time of year, rates are often higher and student discounts are not as common. Try to go during the off-season instead.

Method 2. Getting Deals on Transportation and Lodging

1. Use a ticket aggregator. Ticket aggregators are websites that collect data from a number of travel companies, airlines, hotels, and other travel options. You can then compare the prices side-by-side. To use an aggregator, plug in your dates and destination. You may want to try a few dates to see what deals come up for you.

- If you use a .edu email address for your account on Kayak.com, special deals from StudentUniverse will display alongside other discounted fares.

- Skyscanner.net searches and compares dozens of rates and airfare options. It also offers special advice to student travelers.

2. Buy straight from the airline. Some airlines offer special packages and deals for students. If there is a certain airline that serves your route, you can research to see if they have any specials for students. This can vary greatly based on the time of year, airline, and destination.

- American Airlines offers discounted vacation packages to students with a student ID through their AA Vacations service.

- Lufthansa has special deals and rates for students through their Generation Fly website.

- Low cost airlines such as Ryan Air or Aer Lingus are popular with students for their low-cost flights across Europe. Be aware of extra fees, however, as these can quickly add up.

3. Buy a railcard. Railcards offer discounts to students and young people to reduce the cost of rail travel. While these may have a small upfront fee, you can often make the money after a single trip. Look in your rail company to see if they offer a student rail card.

- Amtrak offers a 15% discount card to students between the ages of 13 and 25.

- In the UK, a 16-25 Railcard can save up to 30% on rail fares for people between the ages of 16 and 25. Full-time students over the age of 25 also qualify.

- Full-time students with an International Student ID card can qualify for unlimited travel in Ontario, Canada through ViaRail.

- Eurail offers a 35% discount to travelers under the age of 25 with a Youth Pass.

4. Find youth hostels. Youth hostels offer cheap accommodations, and they often have many deals for students. Some hostels may even organize special tours or events for student travelers. Read reviews to find a hostel that is both affordable and safe. Signing up for a hostel membership can also save you money.

- In the UK, you can become a member of the Youth Hostel Association. Not only are there special rates for people under 26, but full-time students over the age of 26 can save 10% on a railcard.

- Hostelling International offers a network of safe, clean hostels around the world. By becoming a member, you can save 10% on bookings.

Method 3. Saving Money on Daily Activities

1. Sign up for an international student ID card. The International Student ID card is valid in 120 countries. For many international student discounts, you will only qualify if you can present this

card. By joining, you also gain access to a thousands of discounts on food, shopping, travel, and events.

- The card can take up to four weeks to reach you, so sign up well-before you leave to travel.

- You can apply online at the ISIC website.

2. Ask if there is a student discount. Many museums, landmarks, restaurants, and events offer discounts to students who can present a valid ID card. Wherever you go, you should always ask if they have a student discount.

- You can say, "Hi, do you offer a student discount?" If they don't speak English, you can show them your ID card as you say it, and they will give you the discount if there is one.

- If they have a website listing their entry fees, you might check there first. This can help you plan your trip around cheaper, discounted options.

3. Talk to your hotel. Whether you are staying in a hotel or hostel, you should be able to find some-one who can share their local expertise. Go the front desk, and ask them what student deals are available in the area. They may be able to give you brochures of interesting activities. Some places will even organize their own tours and activities available at special rates.

- You can say, "Hi, I was wondering if knew of any special student deals in this area."

- You can also ask, "Do you plan any special tours or activities for people staying here?"

- If you are staying at a rented apartment or couch surfing, you should ask your host this same question when you first arrive.

Traveling Tips

There are various strategies for having a fruitful and exhilarating travel experience. This chapter provides some useful tips for traveling, such as the correct way to pack for air travel, dress for travel, find cheap accommodation, talk with someone speaking a different language, interact with people from different cultures, etc.

How to Prepare for International Travel

Traveling abroad can be a wonderful experience full of fun, history, and culture. It's important to prepare before you take your trip so that you'll have the best time possible, and avoid mishaps like not being able to charge your cell phone or having your credit card declined. You'll need to plan your trip a few weeks ahead of time to receive your immunizations, passport, and travel visa. You can purchase a guidebook to learn more about the destination country's customs and language.

Method 1. Planning Your Itinerary

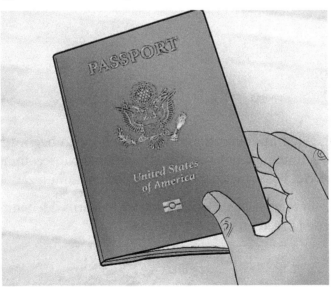

1. Get a passport. You need at least two passport-size photos, your birth certificate, and one other form of identification that proves your citizenship in your country of origin. If you already have a passport, ensure that it has at least 6 months left before its expiration date. Some countries will not issue a visa to you if your passport expires in less than 6 months.

- If you don't already have a passport, you'll need to allow 4-6 weeks for processing, so be sure to start this process ahead of time.

2. Check your destination's visa requirements. If your destination country and country of origin both participate in the Visa Waiver Program, you won't be required to pre-arrange a visa. Other non-participating countries may require you to apply for a tourist visa (and get that visa approved) before you arrive.

- This can be a costly and time-consuming step, so be sure to get it out of the way ahead of time.

- Some countries require that tourists pay entrance and exit fees, so find out if this is applicable to your trip and be prepared to pay the fees.

- U.S. citizens can visit the website for the U.S. Department of State to find out the visa requirements for traveling to foreign countries.

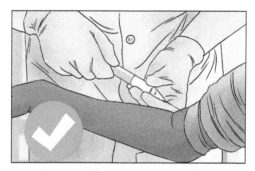

3. Receive the recommended immunizations. You may need to begin immunization injections many months in advance. Immunizations are usually optional but recommended for tourist travel in certain parts of the world. For some countries you need no immunizations at all.

- Check out the Center for Disease Control website to learn which immunizations are recommended or required based on your destination.

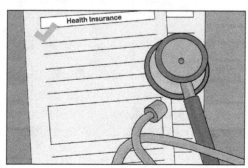

4. Purchase health and travel insurance. If your health insurance policy doesn't cover you while

abroad, it's wise to purchase health insurance that will be accepted in your destination country, just in case something should happen. Similarly, if your trip ends up getting cancelled or postponed, purchasing travel insurance ahead of time can save you money, time, and a lot of hassle.

5. Decide where you will stay. You may choose to stay with friends or relatives, or book a hotel or hostel while on your trip. Though it's possible to make these decisions last-minute, you'll feel more prepared if you have sorted out these details ahead of time. Research places to stay online and read reviews from other guests to find the best spot for your money.

6. Determine the best way to get around. Depending on the location, you may be able to walk, ride a bike, drive a car, or take a boat or train to get around your destination. It's a good idea to look into this beforehand, so you know, for instance, if you'll need a hotel close to the train station, or how to get a ticket for the subway.

- Many countries do not recognize a driver's license from another country, so if you plan to drive while on your trip you'll need to obtain an International Driving Permit. In the U.S., you can do so through AAA or the National Auto Club.

Method 2. Brushing up on International Customs

1. Study the native language. At the very least, you should know a few terms and phrases, such as

"hello," "please," "thank you," "my name is…" "what is your name?" and "where is the bathroom?" The more you can understand and speak the language, the better.

- You can take an introductory language course, purchase language-learning software, or get a language translation book before your trip.

- You can also try a language-learning app, like Duolingo, which is free and perfect for learning on-the-go.

2. Research the local atmosphere. Find an English language newspaper online for the country you are traveling to, then start reading about current events a month or so in advance. Familiarize yourself with sensitive issues.

- You can also find out about special events that may be taking place while you are there.

3. Inquire about the local dress and customs. Do research online or buy a guidebook to help you navigate through these issues. Some countries may be more modest, while others have less restrictions.

- For example, men may get stares if they wear short pants, which may be acceptable only for children in some regions.

- For instance, if you are going to a country where most women dress modestly, you may offend someone by wearing a tank top.

- In other regions, shorts and no top at all might be normal at a beach or sun bathing location.

4. Find out local etiquette to avoid embarrassment. It's important to learn the rules of dress, touch, table manners, and speech before you go to a foreign country. Don't offend your host by hugging upon arrival if that is not acceptable. Likewise, be ready for a kiss upon first meeting where that is expected.

- In some countries it is offensive to touch someone's spouse or children, so keep that in mind.

- It's also important to mind your body language. Find out which hand, head, foot, or face gestures might be offensive or misinterpreted.

- Keep your mind open when things seem shocking or taboo. Be a respectful observer of the local culture, but not a judge.

Method 3. Organizing your Essentials

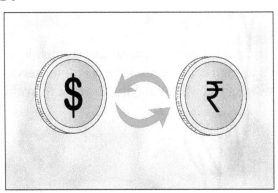

1. Find out the international exchange rate. You can find international exchange rates by searching for currency converters online. For example, you could search "convert Nepalese rupees" to find the rate of that soft currency. Do some calculations and become familiar with what the foreign currency equals in your home currency.

- You should carry some of the local cash on hand, but be sure to use an ATM or visit a bank, rather than paying exorbitant fees at conversion centers in the airport.

- It's also a good idea to see how much things you may need or want (like coffee, a newspaper, a hotel room, a bottle of wine) cost in your destination country so you aren't surprised upon arrival.

2. Research electrical standards in your destination country. Do an Internet search to determine if you may need a plug adapter and a converter. Many online travel sites list the type of plug you need.

- Things that heat up, such as a hair dryer, may not work correctly on the volts and cycles of a foreign country, even with a converter.

- Computer batteries and handheld devices may also be affected by electrical conversion.

3. Notify your bank of your trip. Some banks or credit card companies may decline your card if they aren't aware that you are in a foreign country. Call the customer service center and let them know where you are going and how long you will be staying in order to avoid and delays or declines.

4. Add an international calling plan to your phone service. Many mobile phones will not work in locations other than your home country. Contact your service provider and inquire about international calling plans as well as data rates.

- Alternatively, you can purchase pre-paid calling cards before your trip and use a landline phone, such as in your hotel, to contact friends and family members back home.

- You can also use free communication apps, such as Skype, FaceTime, and/or WhatsApp that use the Internet for phone and video calls as well as text messages.

5. Make copies of your travel documents or itinerary. It's a good idea to make color copies of your passport, plane or train tickets, hotel reservations, etc. If you only have digital copies of your itinerary, you may have trouble accessing them without an Internet connection.

- Keep copies of all your travel documents in your luggage. It's also a good idea to provide a friend or family member with copies in case your luggage gets lost or stolen.

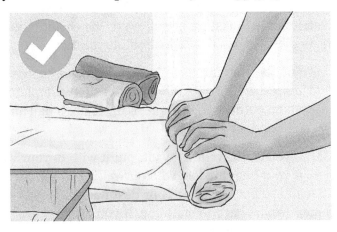

6. Pack wisely. Research the weather, terrain, and airline weight regulations before you travel. Overpacking for international travel is a mistake many people make, but lighter luggage is better. Choose items you really like, and plan on wearing them several times in different combinations.

- Don't forget to bring any medications you may need.

How to Pack for Air Travel

If you've never or infrequently traveled by air, you may be confused and overwhelmed with what to pack. Guidelines seem to get more and more confusing all the time, and now there are sometimes fees to pay? If it's difficult to make sense of, you're not alone. Follow these steps to get it right every time, whether you are flying long, or short haul, for business or for pleasure, this one guide has it all.

Part 1. Packing Your Carry-On

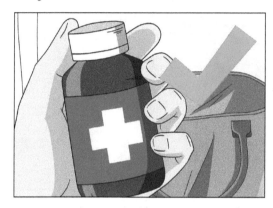

1. If you cannot live without it, pack it in your carry-on. Pack the essentials: undergarments, shoes, a set or two of regular clothes, entertainment, medication and, for longer flights, basic toiletries. Some people fly as if they may never see their luggage again – and that has some merit. Keep in your carry-on the minimum of what you need to survive should you lose your luggage.

- Make sure to take all your medication and everything you need to be comfortable. Prescription and non-prescription medication are allowed. It's easier to get extra liquids through security if they're medically needed, like with saline solution.

- In order to cut down on the amount of clothes to pack, choose items that are interchangeable. Stick to a few items that all go together, rather than completely separate outfits. Use accessories to spice up an outfit. For example, scarves are small and easy to pack, and can be used as a scarf, headband, or even a belt.

- Take your swimsuit if you are travelling by air, put it with in your vacation gear, especially if you are a woman. If your bags are lost when travelling by air, most items (such as shorts or T-shirts) can usually be purchased at your destination. However, if your bags are lost, swimsuits for women can be hard to shop for. If you do not have your swimsuit you may miss out on the beach, hot tub, or other vacation fun.

2. Pack valuables in your carry-on. Anything valuable should come with you in your carry-on. On

the off-chance your luggage gets lost or damaged, your carry on should not leave your possession. If you'd be heartbroken if you lost it, take it in your carry-on if you take it at all.

- Pack large electronics last, so they are easily accessible. You will not need to go digging around when time is of the essence.

3. Pack your electronics together. This is good for two reasons:

- You will probably get bored on your flight, even if it is only half an hour, and having your electronics together lets you know where everything is so you can access your iPod, iPad, Kindle, or whatever else you need as quickly and easily as possible.

- The TSA requires electronics to be screened – when they are all in the same place and easy for the agents to see, you won't be the one holding up the line at security.

4. Make sure you have your documents. In order to get on the plane, you need identification, such as a passport or driver's license. Do not forget your ATM card and credit card or AAA card. However, it is probably a good idea NOT to take every piece of plastic you own because you run the risk of losing the cards.

- In an easily accessible pocket of your carry-on luggage, store your flight information: the airline, the flight number, your confirmation code, and the flight details. This comes in handy at the self-service check-in kiosks that so many airlines provide now at the airport.

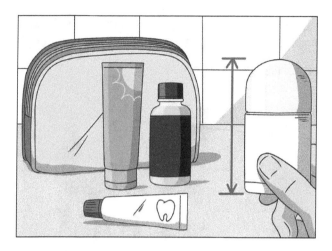

5. Do you really need toiletries? You may not need to pack much, if any. Your Aunt Maria probably has shampoo, for instance, and Peru will likely have toothpaste. It may take an extra stop at a store on your travels, but by avoiding tons of bottles, lotions, and tubes, you save space for other, more important things.

- If you do bring toiletries, in the United States the 3-1-1 TSA regulations still applies. You can fill as many 3 oz bottles of toiletries (100 ml) as you want into "one" quart-size plastic ziplock bag (limit one per flyer), but you have to take out the bag at security screening. Go to www.tsa.gov for the full rules and regulations.

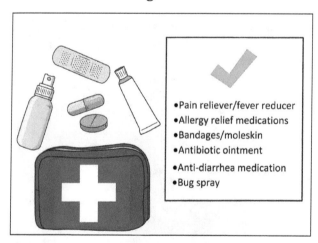

- Have a first aid kit with the basics, especially pain medication. Sometimes flights can cause headaches, so have a pack ready just in case this happens to be that one. A few things you may want to pack:

- Painkillers

- Bandages

- A sedative (if you are a nervous traveler)

- Anti-nausea medication

- Chewing gum (for air pressure changes)

- Tissues

- Earplugs (good for travel in general)

- Medication for anything you are prone to, such as allergies.

6. Wear it, do not pack it. Remember you are not charged for the clothes you wear traveling, so dress with that in mind. Dress in layers so you can bring more with you. Instead of a T-shirt and jacket, wear a T-shirt under a long sleeved top under a sweatshirt, for example. Wear your hiking shoes and pack your flip-flops, especially when you are travelling for business.

Part 2. Packing Your Checked Luggage

1. Avoid checking luggage if you can. You can manage, which earn traveling by air, for a three month work trip, without checking any bags if you really want to. Checking luggage, for some, is a pain in the rear. You have to worry about packing it, dragging it with you, meeting weight requirements, likely paying extra fees that you did not know about, and then hoping the airlines do not lose it. If you are traveling for less than two weeks, consider it. It may be a challenge, but it is doable.

- Flight attendants and crew do it all the time. They can go over a week with just a carry on. If they can do it, so can you. You can then use the extra $50, if applicable, for whatever you please.

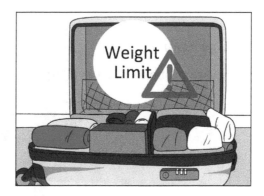

2. Pack as light as possible. In addition to meeting the weight requirements, it's just easier to pack lighter – fewer things may get lost (via flying or when you leave them in your hotel room), it is a lighter bag to tote around, and you'll have plenty of room for souvenirs and impulse buys. And it'll take less time to repack.

- Though you should hold off on bringing too many shoes, you have to bring some. Shoe should be packed in plastic bags to avoid soiling your others goods unless they are brand new. Also, consider packing socks in your shoes rather than waste space.

3. Put copies of your important documents in your checked luggage. Just in case something were to happen to your carry on, you forget to pack your carry-on correctly, or something unfortunate happens on your trip, put copies of important documents in your checked luggage. Scan your passport, visa, and anything else that you may need in the worst of circumstances. If you do it, you won't need it. But if you don't, you may.

4. Expect bottles to leak when you travel by air. If you are bringing toiletries with you, it is likely

something will leak. Each item should be wrapped separately and stored in bags to make sure none of it gets on your clothes. Keep these in a separate area in your bag, too.

- Take the lid off of each bottle and plastic wrap the top; then put the lid back on. This means that even if the lid opens, you should still be fine.

5. Roll your clothes. If you are not already rolling your clothes, get on the bandwagon. It prevents awkward square-shaped wrinkles and it saves room, so hop to it. Start with the heavier ones on bottom as lighter ones are generally more moldable to the shape of the top of your bag.

- The tighter the roll, the more room you save. Even a little more compression here and there goes a long way.

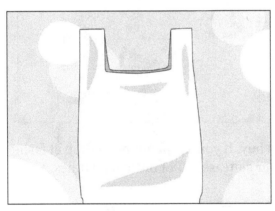

6. Take an extra plastic bag or two. Some airports are courteous enough to provide plastic bags for you, but if yours is not one of those, take them yourself. They are always useful, especially if you are traveling in a group – someone always forgets. And this way if your first round bags get soiled, you have a backup.

- The zipper kind – the kind that literally has a zipper on it. The resealable ones are better than the non-sealable kind, but the zipper kind are best – the resealable kind can open when force is applied.

- High-quality zip-lock bags can also be used to pack your bag tighter. You can sometimes get to 1/3 more room if your clothing is put in zip-lock bags, the air forced out, then sealed. It can also protect clothing from getting soaked in outdoor adventures and keep your dirty underwear away from your clean clothes.

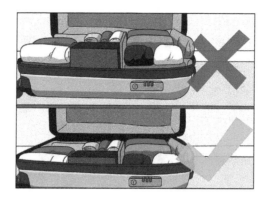

7. Play tetris with your belongings. To get the most out of your bag, you've gotta pack it according to shape and size of your items. Start with the biggest, heaviest items on bottom and work your way up to the light items – this will make it easier to close your bag when all is said and done. If something is an odd shape, pack clothes around it – make it a point to never pack air.

• In general, it's easier to back long, cylindrical items than odd shaped bottles and containers. In the future, to streamline your packing look for items that are of more basic shapes and sizes. They take up less room overall.

8. Do not pack what you will buy. If you are planning to shop at fashionable Parisian boutiques on your travels, do not stuff your suitcase full of ordinary clothes. Leave room for your purchases in your bags.

9. Can you ship ahead? In some cases, it may be easier to ship your items by mail or by a service like FedEx or UPS. This may be very important if you are going on an extended trip or need special equipment, like winter camping gear.

Part 3. Preparing for Your Trip

1. Know the duration of your flight and trip. Your trip destination will determine the kinds of things to pack, and the length will determine how much of each item is to be packed. What days do you have special events planned? How can you use the same pieces over and over?

- If you can, try to avoid needing a checked bag. More and more airlines are charging for that first checked bag, and a cheap flight can turn into an expensive one in a matter of no time. If flight attendants can live out of a carry-on for over a week at a time, so can you.

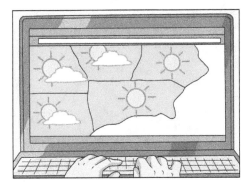

2. Check the weather. Checking before packing can help pinpoint what you really need. For example, Vermont typically has mild summers, but also has "heat waves" that can make it semi-tropical. Checking the weather will let you know if you really need to pack that tank top or that umbrella.

- Take a small amount of multipurpose items to deal with the climate of your vacation destination. For instance, one waterproof windbreaker takes less space than a raincoat and a jacket.

3. If you are leaving your country, check if you need adapters. If you're going to a different country or overseas, odds are certain things will be different. Will you need an electronics adapter?

4. Understand prohibitions. You may not be able to bring your Saudi host a bottle of wine, for example. Or take certain kinds of plant seeds to Australia.

How to Dress for Airplane Travel

Let's face it, nobody wants to wear their best outfit on a stuffy, overcrowded airplane. All most people want to wear is something comfy but chic. So if you want tips on dressing to fly, read on

Steps

1. Dress with practicality in mind. The airport not a catwalk. Airports and airplanes are full of tired holidaymakers who have no desire to look their very best. You can look clean cut and fashionable without wearing your best outfit.

2. Mix and match. You could wear your comfiest, maybe slightly worn bottoms and your favourite, more dressy top. Or vice versa. Your whole outfit doesn't have to be high fashion, but one piece could be.

3. Wear a comfy outfit and dressier accessories, like a fashionable carry on bag or nice jewellery.

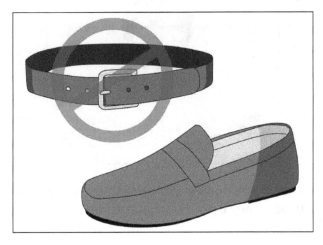

4. Try to think about things like going through security. If you can avoid it, don't wear a belt as you'll have to take it off. Wear shoes that are easy to take off and put back on, not the ones that take ages to lace up.

5. Don't wear awkward things like high heels, as stepping onto the plane might be pretty tricky and you'll have less chance of escape if you have to get out in a hurry.

6. Wearing or carrying things with offensive slogans or images isn't recommended. You might not get an easy time from other passengers if you're wearing a t-shirt with a racist joke or a picture of a middle finger. There will be thousands of different people with different beliefs, be respectful of that.

7. Wear a tracksuit and trainers if you don't want to use these tips. Nobody will judge you for looking slightly sloppier than usual. They'll be too busy rushing around to know or care what other passengers are wearing.

How to Travel Comfortably on a Long Flight

Do you have trouble with packing, airport security, or that scratchy pillow wrapped in plastic? If so, this topic has some helpful tips on how to manage an overnight plane ride.

Steps

1. Wear comfortable leggings with a loose shirt. When you get off of the plane, you will look cute.

You can throw a pair of fuzzy socks in your carry-on bag. Also, you might want to check to make sure you aren't wearing any belts, headbands, or hair ties with a metal band.

2. Do smart packing. You will most likely need a suitcase and a carry on bag.

- Use a website that lets you check off what you need and it will print out your personal packing list. Make sure to include pants, shirts, rain jackets, socks, underwear, cosmetics and toiletries, and any chargers you may need. If you are traveling to Europe, for example, you need an outlet converter so that you can charge your phone.

How to Find a Cheap Motel or Hotel

Finding inexpensive accommodations may take a bit of work, but it is possible.

Steps

1. Get a travel guide for your destination. Publishers like Rough Guide, Let's Go and Lonely Planet usually write travel books targeted to younger (read: poorer) travelers and include lists of cheap places to stay.

2. Check out Hostelling International online. They run affordable, comfortable hostels worldwide.

3. See if there is a YWCA or YMCA at your destination that provides beds for travelers.

4. Some schools offer accommodations to their alumni, such as the Harvard Club, the worldwide network of Sacred Heart schools etc. Check to see if your college does the same.

5. Try discount travel sites like Orbitz, Travelocity etc.

6. Subscribe to weekly travel discount online mailing lists such as Sherman's or Travelzoo.

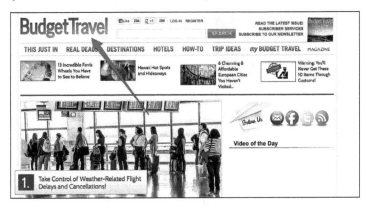

7. Read Arthur Frommer's Budget Travel.

8. Google "cheap hotels [name of destination]".

9. Look at travel blogs and travel wikis.

How to Talk With Someone Who Doesn't Speak your Language

With hundreds of languages in the world, it's not uncommon to encounter a language barrier during your work, travel, or everyday life. Talking to someone who doesn't speak the same language as you can certainly be challenging. With a little patience and some creativity, however, it is possible to communicate with someone, regardless of whether or not you speak the same language.

Method 1. Communicating Verbally

1. Determine whether there is any possibility of verbal communication. Your first step should be to determine whether you and the person you are talking to know any of the same words. Even a few basic words can help, whether you can understand a few terms in their language or vice versa.

- If you recognize their language and you know a few words, that's great. If not, ask if the other person understands any English.

- English is the language of travel and business. It is likely that even in parts of the world education is not widespread, many people will still know a few words or phrases in English.

- If that fails, try any other languages you know, even if you only understand a little bit. See if the other person shows any signs of understanding. Just a few words can make communication much easier, even if they're not in either of your native tongues.

2. Speak slowly. If it seems there is a chance the other person will understand even few words, try speaking to them in English (or any other language both you and he or she understand a little) very slowly. Slowing down will make it easier for him or her to understand.

- That said, try to keep a normal rhythm. When you slow down your speech, you may have a tendency to get into an odd, stilted rhythm and/or put emphasis on the wrong words. This can make you harder to understand.

- If you speak English with a strong regional accent (e.g. you live in the deep south or have cockney accent), speaking slowly is doubly important.

3. Don't shout. Many people have a tendency to raise their voices when talking to someone who doesn't speak their language, or doesn't speak it well. This isn't actually helpful. Avoid doing this.

- Shouting will only make you look foolish and may offend the person you are trying to communicate with.

4. Keep your words simple. Use the simplest words you can to express yourself. Definitely stay away from any jargon, technical language, or similarly complex words.

- Likewise, stay away from the use of idioms or figures of speech. These are expressions that, by definition, are culturally specific, and are not likely to be understood by non-English speakers.

- For example, don't say something is "as easy as pie" or that you you need to "hit the sack." These common American expressions obviously don't have meanings that align with the literal meaning of the words. They are likely to seem bizarre and perplexing to non-native English speakers.

5. Beware of challenging phrases. Similarly, use the simplest sentence structures you can. Use as few words as possible to get your meaning across.

- Avoid confusing structures, such as questions asked in the negative. Instead of saying: "You don't have any idea what I mean, do you?" ask "Do you understand what I mean?"

6. Be consistent. Once you've chosen a word for something, don't switch to another term for same thing. This can add confusion and create misunderstandings.

- For example, if you are trying to ask where you can buy some pain medication, stick with that term, don't vary your words and say "aspirin" or "painkillers" or some other synonym a moment later, at least not if the person you are talking to seemed to understand the first term.

7. Listen actively. Ask questions to make sure the other person is understanding you, and express your understanding when he or she successfully communicates something to you.

- Similarly, be on lookout for signals that she or he does not understand you, such a scrunched brow or the universal "huh?"

8. Put it in writing. Many people who are just learning English understand things better in written form than via spoken language. If speaking isn't working, it might be worth writing down a few words.

- This also eliminates problems that might come about because of pronunciation issues, especially if you have a strong accent.

- Carrying a small notepad and pen for this purpose when you travel is a good idea.

9. Be patient and polite. Interactions with someone who doesn't speak your language can be frustrating, both for you and the other person. Be as patient as you can, and try to keep your frustration to yourself.

- Do not laugh at the person, roll your eyes, or anything else that you wouldn't do in polite conversation with someone who does speak your language.

10. Get a foreign language dictionary or phrasebook. If you are traveling to a country where English isn't common, it's good idea to pick up a dictionary and/or phrasebook that will help you understand and speak a few words and phrases in the dominant language.

- While a dictionary will give you a greater variety of words to choose from, a phrase book will contain useful sentences with the verbs already conjugated correctly. This can make you easier for others to understand.

- Small dictionary/phrasebook combinations are available for travelers via your local bookstore or online.

- Some travel guidebooks including a section of common phrases as well.

Method 2. Using Other Means of Communication

1. Use gestures. Whether the person you are trying to communicate with can understand a single word you are saying or not, simple gestures can often be helpful in reinforcing meanings or conveying basic ideas. Use gestures such as pointing at objects that are almost universally understood.

- Using your hands to indicate size, location, and so on can be very helpful.

- Be careful, not all gestures are universal. Some common gestures in America have very different meanings in other places. For example, the common sign for "ok" or "perfect" made by touching the tips of your thumb and forefinger is an offensive gesture in Greece and Turkey. So keep it simple.

2. Act it out. While it might seem silly, sometimes you can communicate by acting out what you are trying to communicate, like in a game of charades. People might laugh at you, but if you can get your point across, it's probably worth it.

- For example, if you are trying to find a good place to eat, you might act out the motion taking some bites with a fork, then rub your belly and and make a contented sound, such as "Mmmmm."

3. Draw a picture. If you're carrying a notepad and pen or pencil, you may be able to communicate effectively by drawing things. Looking for the bus station? Try doing a quick sketch of a bus.

- You can pass the pad off to the other person and let them respond using a picture too, if that helps.

4. Use an app. If you have a smart phone and access to the internet, there are numerous translation apps you can use to make conversation easier. Many of these allow you to simply talk into the phone and will translate what you've said to the language of your choice.

- Some of these apps are free. It's a good idea to download one before going on a trip somewhere where English isn't spoken.

How to Learn about other Cultures

Learning about other cultures is an invaluable experience. Gaining an understanding of other cultures benefits both you and other people by deepening your understanding of how different people live. There are many ways to attain knowledge about other cultures. You can do research via the internet or local library, get to know other cultures in your community, and travel whenever possible.

Method 1. Utilizing Technology for Research

1. Read online news sources. Choose what culture or cultures you would like to learn more about. Subscribe to newspapers from that culture online to know more about what they are reading. Browse websites with data on entertainment, outings, politics, or trends.

- You should be able to find news sources from different cultures in your language. You don't have to learn the language at first to get to know more about the culture, although learning the language will be helpful eventually.

- For example, search for "French news in English."

2. Follow social media about your chosen culture. A great thing about the internet is that it has made the world smaller and more accessible than ever. You can find people from cultures all around the world on Facebook, Twitter, Instagram, etc. Following people or organizations from other cultures on social media is a great way to directly learn from that culture about things like their values, cuisine, and fashion.

- You can be specific when looking up information about other cultures on social media. Search for the accounts of notable figures in that culture, or look up webpages dedicated to specific parts of that culture, such as fashion, entertainment, art, or politics.

3. Ask questions online. There are plenty of ways to ask questions about a culture online directly to members of that culture. Take a look at local communities and forums that accept questions or conversations. Send in or post a question and wait for a response.

- Ask what daily life is like in their culture.

- You can ask what current events are going on right now, and how or if it is having an effect on them.

- Ask what the major holidays are like there, and how they celebrate them.

- Always be careful when communicating with other people online. Don't give away your personal information.

- Be respectful when asking questions. Research your question before asking.

4. Look up YouTube videos. YouTube is another form of social media that allows passive watching or interaction. There are many channels on YouTube dedicated to a specific culture or aspects of a culture. Often, these videos are produced by people that come from that culture, or know a lot about it.

- Type into the YouTube search bar things such as "Learn about French culture," or "What do people in India commonly eat?"

- Many YouTube channels talk about subjects like news, history, or gender norms. Search for videos with a specific subject in mind.

- You can ask questions in the comment sections of YouTube videos, but responses from knowledgeable sources are not guaranteed.

5. Get a pen or email pal. Exchanging with a pen pal is a great way to learn about another culture from someone who is living in that culture. You can learn about language, daily life, and parts of the culture that you may not find from doing research online. Technology has made it possible to write letters, emails, or even video chat with a pen pal.

- Search for verifiable pen pal programs online. It is better to go through a program rather than finding a pen pal yourself.

- Never give away more information than necessary to your pen pal.

Method 2. Taking a Trip to the Library

1. Visit the library and check out travel books. Reading through travel books and travel journals gives you great ideas about local and international destinations and begins to expose you to new cultures.

- You can check out a guide to your chosen culture, or read travel journals by people who have spent time in that culture.

- Look for guides that cover information about etiquette, gender roles, festivals, and religion.

2. Read books written by people from other cultures. You can read fiction, nonfiction, poetry, or anything written by a person from the culture you want to learn about. Reading books by people from other cultures gives you a glimpse into the mind and life of the people from that culture that would be difficult to obtain otherwise.

- Ask your librarian for recommendations, or search online for famous books from that culture.

- Read a history book about the culture you want to learn more about. It is important to know information on subjects such as major conflicts, holidays, and customs.

- If the culture has a different language than your native language, search for translations of books in your language.

3. Check out films from other cultures. Most libraries have a section where you can check out videos. Ask your librarian if any foreign films are available. Look for videos that offer translations or subtitles. Films from other cultures offer a view of what that culture values as entertainment.

- If your library does not offer foreign films, search online for where to order or rent foreign films.

- Also look for documentaries about other cultures. A documentary may not be produced by people from that culture, but often they are produced by people knowledgeable about the culture.

4. Search for a language guide. Most libraries will have books that either give a basic overview of a language, or serve as a textbook. Learning the language of the culture you want to know more about is one of the best ways to get to know the culture.

- Look for a book specifically for beginners if you are new to the language.

Method 3. Getting Involved in your Local Community

1. Volunteer to practice your language with others. Offer help to people in your community who speak your language as a second language. Search for schools or organizations in your community that ask for volunteer teachers, or offer to help people at school, church, or other parts of your community that are trying to learn your language. In exchange for practicing English, you can ask to learn more about their culture and language.

- Commit to helping just as much, if not more, than you are receiving information.

2. Visit local museums and cultural centers. Museums will often have exhibitions about other cul-

tures. Ask museums in your area about current or upcoming exhibitions. Also, check with cultural centers in your area for opportunities to learn about cultures outside of your own.

- Many museums have online exhibitions if you do not have that many museums in your area.

3. Enroll in a class. Many community colleges allow enrollment for individual courses. You can take a language course, or a course specifically about a certain culture. Contact local colleges and teaching institutions in your area for more information about classes.

- Make sure you have time to commit to a class that may require homework and tests.

- A class will probably require money. Look up information or ask local institutions about course requirements and cost.

4. Make friends in your community. It is always good to make friends from other cultures. It is a way to gain compassion and understanding, as well as possibly gaining a valuable friendship. Reach out to people in your community from work, school, or other local organizations.

- Talk to them about how your culture differs from their own. Ask what the biggest differences has been for them.

- Offer your companionship to people, but never force yourself on anyone that is unwilling to communicate.

- Be respectful of a potential friend's culture. Do not say any slurs, or act in a manner that is disrespectful to their culture.

- Become friends for the right reasons. Wish to gain knowledge about their culture, but don't use a person only to benefit from information.

5. Search for cultural experiences in your community. There are probably more opportunities to educate yourself on other cultures in your community than you realize. Look for ethnic restaurants, places of worship, and ask about upcoming festivals or holidays. Ask first before entering a place of worship or inviting yourself to a celebration.

- Express that you are genuinely interested in their culture, and do not want to disrespect it in any way.

6. Avoid cultural appropriation. Ask members of your community from other cultures, or search online to ask about appropriate behavior and dress. It is important to be respectful, but do not appropriate another person's culture. Avoid cultural appropriation by asking questions, such as:

- What behaviors and styles make you uncomfortable when people from other cultures exhibit them?

- Why is this food or artifact important to your culture?

- Is it okay to join in on this festival or celebration?

- How do I show appropriately show respect to your culture?

Method 4. Traveling When Possible

1. Take part in an exchange program. Some schools or churches have opportunities to take part in an exchange program. In these programs, you often trade places with a person from another culture. You will typically live with another family, go to school or work in their area, and integrate yourself with the community.

- Ask for more information from your school, church, or reputable website offering exchange programs.

- Most of these programs require money. Consider fundraising or saving money for the trip.

2. Volunteer abroad. There many opportunities to travel abroad through volunteer programs. There are several types of volunteer programs. Some programs require you to teach English, some want farm workers, and other programs ask for humanitarian aid.

- Some programs require you to pay for your own trip, but others will pay for your services, as well as room and board. Make sure you know what is required before signing up for any program.

- Volunteer for the right reasons. You will gain valuable knowledge about another culture through volunteering, but make sure you are willing to dedicate yourself to helping others.

3. Go on a road trip. If you do not have money for air travel, take a road trip. Depending on your location, you can drive as far as another country, or to another state. You do not to drive far to experience a culture that is at least slightly different from your own.

- Plan a road trip that will take you through multiple towns, states, or even countries.

4. Save money for travel. Traveling is the best way to learn about other cultures. Firsthand experience is the most definitive way gain knowledge and experience. Traveling can be expensive, so plan your trip far ahead of time.

- Do your research through the internet, library, or local community before you travel.

- Make sure that the place you want to travel to is safe, and obtain the correct documents for travel specific to that region.

How to be Culturally Sensitive when Traveling Abroad

Travel is an extraordinary thing. But when you're visiting a different country for the first time, there's always a risk of offending the native population by failing to observe customs that are normal for them, or by not being aware of aspects of your own culture that might be considered rude or out of place. Few things are more embarrassing than disrupting someone's way of life simply because you don't know any better. Whenever you set off to see the world on a globe-spanning adventure, keep in mind the unique values and social climate of the culture you're immersing yourself in, and think about how your behavior might be perceived by those around you.

Part 1. Experiencing Different Cultures

1. Educate yourself on the place you're visiting. Before you even step foot on a plane, conduct some rigorous research to help you prepare for your first encounter with a new country and its people. It will be worth finding out about your destination's social structure, religious practices and attitude toward foreign travelers. Reading up on where you're headed is a must, as it will offer valuable insight into daily life there and give you an idea of what to expect as an outsider.

- For a casual vacation to the South of France, you might only need to look into acceptable dinner attire, whereas a work trip to Japan or the Netherlands should be prefaced with some investigation into how leaders there ordinarily conduct formal business.

- Peruse travel blogs written by other visitors from around the world to get their take on a particular place.

2. Reflect on your own culture and behaviors. How is the culture you come similar to that of the place you're traveling to? How is it different? Look at yourself through someone else's eyes and take note of values and characteristics that may set you apart from those around you. You might, for example, identify as a feminist and be headed for a place where women traditionally occupy

a marginalized role in society. Try not to let culture clashes influence your attitude. Make it your mission to present the best of yourself and where you're from to others while you're away.

- Remember that you'll be representing your home country while abroad, even on casual pleasure trips.

- Be especially mindful when traveling to places that have been embroiled in conflict with your place of origin.

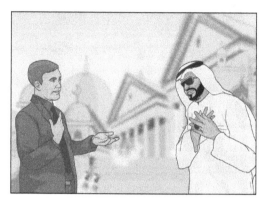

3. Appreciate differences. The culture that you'll be stepping into won't be the same as your own, and that's a good thing. Diversity is a quality that should be embraced. You might feel uncomfortable in a given cultural setting at first, but with an open mind you'll start to see just how truly colorful and astounding the world can be.

- Let go of any stereotypes or generalizations about the place you're visiting.

- Using a squatting toilet or being warned against sitting with your legs crossed in Turkey might catch you off guard, but gaining a deeper understanding of these types practices is probably the one of the reasons you're traveling in the first place.

Part 2. Conducting yourself in Unfamiliar Surroundings

1. Try to blend in with those around you. As a traveler, you'll be in someone else's backyard, which means you have an unspoken obligation to abide by their way of life. With this in mind, your behavior should be modest and in keeping with that of your native counterparts. This means being polite, considerate and eager to make a good impression without trying to show off or make light of your new environment.

- Keep your voice at a respectable volume in public places. Avoid shouting, cursing or doing anything that might cause a scene.

- Know what the norms are when it comes to things like alcohol and tobacco use, photography and other forms expression.

2. Learn to speak the language. Though not a must, it can be extremely helpful to learn a few choice words and phrases in the local dialect. Not only is speaking another language a practical skill, as it will help you find your way around, it shows that you're taking a genuine interest in the culture. This will allow you to forge more meaningful connections with the people you interact with.

- Memorize the names of important objects and places first, like the hotel, bathroom or cafe, to better orient yourself with the area.

- Bring along a phrasebook, or use an app like DuoLingo or Rosetta Stone to polish your handling of a foreign tongue.

- If nothing else, learn to say "please," "thank you" and other basic courtesies. In many cultures, this is a sign of good faith that you're making an effort.

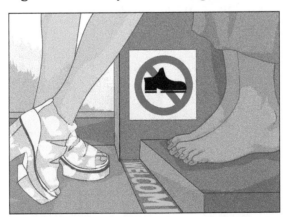

3. Respect local laws and customs. Knowing how to act on foreign soil, and how not to act, can keep you from landing in hot water with the local people and authorities. For instance, it is customary in some parts of the world to greet someone with a bow or a kiss on the cheek rather than a handshake, or for couples to refrain from excessive displays of affection in public places. It's important to abide by these regulations, even if you don't understand or agree with them.

- Some more peculiar types of laws have come to be termed "tourist traps" because of their tendency to get unsuspecting travelers in trouble. Some examples of these include a chewing gum ban in Singapore and a law prohibiting motorists from stopping for pedestrians in Beijing.

- Take off your shoes before entering any private residence in Japan, Russia, Finland, Turkey or Switzerland.

4. Avoid offending the people around you. While you're carrying out your preliminary research, be sure to look up a list of "don'ts" for the area you'll be staying in. In the Middle East, India and some parts of Africa, for example, it's impolite to offer your left hand for a handshake due to that hand's association with unclean sanitary activities. Being informed will keep you from making an unfortunate faux pas.

- Be mindful not to touch anyone's head in countries where Buddhism is practiced or point the soles of your feet at anyone in Arabian cultures, as these are clear signs of disrespect.

- Innocent hand gestures like the thumbs up, peace sign or "A-OK" motion may have vulgar alternative meanings depending on where you go.

- If you happen to offend someone inadvertently, apologize sincerely and gently remind them that you didn't know any better.

5. Be prepared to tip. Familiarize yourself with the particular country's tipping customs when eating out or hitching a ride. In some parts of the world, including Australia, Costa Rica and most of Europe, tipping is neither required nor expected. Everywhere else it is often extended as a gesture of gratitude. Remember that members of other professions, like rickshaw drivers and hotel por-

ters, survive on tips as well, not just waiters.

- When in doubt, leave a modest but customary tip of 15% of the bill's total at dining establishments. Always tip using the local currency, if you can.

- Tipping in Japan and Korea may be construed as an insult.

6. Watch how you dress. Most people are used to wearing whatever they please, but other parts of the world that are more conservative may have different standards for their inhabitants. Observe the style of dress of those around you and aim to approximate their appearance and avoid upsetting others with impolite displays. As a general rule, you should clad yourself modestly and avoid clothing with slogans or imagery that may be considered offensive.

- When visiting a temple, mosque or other place of worship, it's a good idea to dress simply and unostentatiously and be careful about wearing clothing that shows too much skin. Women should be prepared to cover their heads at Islamic religious sites.

- Many cultures, from the United Arab Emirates to Spain, have laws against public nudity and indecency. Save swimwear and other revealing outfits for the beaches.

Part 3. Getting the Most Out of Your Travels

1. Interact with the locals. If you want to discover what makes a place special, make it a point to engage with those who call it home. Get out and live among the people rather than just passively observing them. Your taxi driver or tour guide can tell you things that no map can.

- Do your best to appear in control at all times. Making it obvious that you're a tourist in over your head can make you an easy target.

- Stop and ask someone when you need help or directions instead of relying on your mobile device.

- Make new friends and have them show you around during your stay for a more intimate and authentic experience of the culture.

2. Absorb everything you can. In many ways, traveling is the ultimate teacher. You have a rare chance to dive in headfirst and see so many new and astonishing things firsthand, and to learn about what makes life interesting in the process. Capture new sights on camera, or keep a travel journal to record the details of your adventures. Take advantage of this chance to enrich yourself.

- Take part in local cultural events like the Mardi Gras in French New Orleans, Germany's Oktoberfest or the Songkran Water Festival in Thailand.

- A stacked itinerary will not only keep you busy but allow you to get better acquainted with unique character of a given culture.

3. Get out of your comfort zone. Traveling is every bit as much about doing and feeling as it is witnessing. Go hang-gliding in the Alps or sign up for salsa lessons in Brazil. Don't be afraid to put yourself out there and experience everything a culture has to offer, from its history and politics to its charming and unusual quirks.

- Write down a list of specific things you want to see and do, or challenge yourself to try one new thing every day.

- It's normal to feel like you're in over your head at first. This can be a very good thing, as it means you're able to recognize and appreciate cultural disparities. If you wanted to be completely comfortable at all times, you could just as easily stay home.

4. Stay positive. There are many times when traveling can become a source of frustration, especially when you're lost somewhere halfway around the world where no one speaks the same language. But nothing can cure a sour outlook like a smile. No matter what happens, keep a cool head and a positive attitude and be grateful for the opportunity to see more of the world.

- A happy, confident demeanor will make you more approachable, and make it less likely for scheming opportunists to try to take advantage of you.

- Inconveniences happen: you'll get lost, run low on money or encounter a frustrating language barrier. What's important is that you don't let unforeseen mishaps keep you from falling in love with new places.

CHAPTER 5

World Travel

Traveling the world requires careful planning, scheduling and budgeting. This chapter is a comprehensive guide on world travel. It addresses some important ways to make traveling across the globe including South America, Canada, United States, Germany, Switzerland and the UK an easy task.

How to Travel the World

Traveling the world is an enriching way to expand your knowledge of other cultures, find new work experiences, and gain unique educational insights. However, it can also be expensive, and unprepared travelers can soon find themselves in over their heads. World travel takes planning, frugality, and an independent spirit. Through careful planning both before your trip, and when you're on the road, you can have an enjoyable international travel experience.

Part 1. Planning Ahead for your Travel

1. Decide where to travel. The world is a big place, and there are many, many different places you can visit. Decide if you want to spend all of your time in a single country, a single continent, or if you truly want to travel over the entire globe. It can be helpful to start your international travel in a location you've been to before, and branch out further from there.

- Certain countries (especially in Asia) can be less expensive for Western travelers, although they may lack some of the amenities that we've grown used to.

- Certain regions are also better set up to accommodate tourists and travelers, by offering hostels and other accommodations. (For example, New Zealand is well set up for travelers, while Japan is less so.)

- However, if you're looking for a more adventurous travel experience and want to avoid places most international travelers visit, you may want to plan to visit less accommodating destinations.

2. Make a travel schedule. Before you jump on a plane, train, or ship, you'll need to have at least a rough idea of where you'll be going and how long you'll spend at each destination. It can be easy for a worldwide vacation to take more time than anticipated, so try to set out as specific of a schedule as possible before you leave. Alternately, some people prefer to leave their travel open-ended, and to only plan one week and one destination into the future.

- How long do you want your trip to be? Your schedule will be dramatically different if you want to travel the world for a month, 6 months, or a full year.

- Plan ahead for how your world travel will fit into your life back home. Are you going to quit your job, or will your employer allow you to work while you travel?

3. Research the country (or countries) you'll be traveling to. Do your homework about histories and current events in each country you plan to visit when you travel across the world. This will help you be aware of any local customs you need to follow and any conflicts or dangerous areas of the country you should avoid.

- If you know any individuals in a country you'll be traveling too (even if they're only the friend of a friend), get in touch and ask them about any disruptive political or cultural events that may interfere with your travel plan.

4. Budget for your international travel. The expense of round-the-world travel is a major deterrent for many people. In addition to the plane tickets and other travel fees, you will need to pay for food and lodging, both of which quickly become expensive. Plan this out (as much as possible) ahead of time, so that you can limit your spending and will not be unpleasantly surprised by your expenditures once your trip has ended.

- Start planning well ahead of time and decide how you're going to fund your trip. For example, if you're going to pay for everything out of a savings account, you may need to work extra hours for months on end to fund your travel.

- A general rule of thumb is to try not to exceed $50 a day (not including air fare.)

- Avoid expensive travel options within a country; travel by foot or local transportation whenever possible, and keep an eye out for budget-friendly airline or train options.

- Unless eating in restaurants when you travel is important to you, avoid them. Restaurants quickly become expensive, and you can buy groceries and cook your meals for much less money.

- Put a cap on your spending: an amount that you absolutely cannot exceed, and make sure that your budget doesn't put you over that amount.

5. Let your travel pay for itself. If you have the time and interest, you may be able to travel extremely inexpensively by either uniting your travel goals and your employment, or by taking a few cost-cutting measures for lodging.

- Work for an international teaching organization. Operations like the EKIP Program allow you to teach English overseas for an extended period of time, often with the majority of your expenses paid.

- Stay at hostels when you travel. Hostels are inexpensive, generally safe environments to spend a few nights in while you're traveling.

- Work on a cruise ship. These are built to travel, and you'll be generating an income at the same time.

Part 2. Planning the Specifics of your Trip

1. Learn some universal phrases. It would be a huge undertaking to learn the language of each country you want to visit when you travel the world, but you can make traveling easier by memorizing a few key phrases in each country's language to help you communicate with the locals and get around. Learn how to:

- Greet and thank someone.

- How to agree and disagree (a polite "yes" or "no").

- How to ask how much money something costs.

- How to ask where a place is located (the bathroom, the library, a restaurant, the airport or train station, etc.).

2. Compare methods of travel ahead of time. You will likely have the option of traveling by ship,

train, or airplane. All of these methods will have multi-country ticket plans. Price out around-the-world ticket packages for the countries you want to visit so you can choose the most economical form of travel.

- Although financial saving may be your main goal, also consider the speed and safety of the methods of travel you are considering.

3. Update your passport. Traveling to other countries requires you to have a valid passport. Planning to start traveling the world will be much easier and more efficient if you have this well ahead of time.

- The passport application process can take 4 to 6 weeks to complete, so give yourself a few months before you plan to travel in order to acquire this documentation.

- If you do not have a passport, the best place to look for instruction is online. There are online forms you can fill out to receive your passport.

- You can also fill out and submit the passport paperwork at your local post office.

4. Get a visa, if necessary. Certain countries will require you to have a travel visa before entering, while others only need to see a passport. (For example, American citizens do not need a travel visa to enter the EU.) The document will specify your reason for being in a country, and how long you anticipate staying. In addition, different countries have distinct visas, and you will need a separate visa for each visa-requiring country you travel to.

- Some visas last for more time than others. Check before you start traveling. You'll need to know if your visa lasts for five years, three years, or only one year.

- Check the U.S. State Department website to see if you need a travel visa for your intended destination. The State Department can also provide the paperwork you'll fill out to apply for a visa.

5. Update your immunizations. Although this is not a glamorous part of the travel process, it will benefit you immensely. Foreign countries may have different diseases from those you could contract in your native country, so it's best to inform your doctor of every region you'll be traveling to and ask which immunizations they recommend.

- Be sure to heed any travel health warnings in the countries you'll be visiting. Always check local and national health warnings before traveling to a new region.

- Be sure to pack any prescription or over-the-counter medications you need, since these could be difficult to acquire overseas.

Part 3. Travelling Intelligently and Effectively

1. Pack as conservatively as possible for your world travel. You should bring only essentials in your luggage. Heavy luggage and multiple bags will only weight you down and increase the cost of your travel.

- Bring sturdy, comfortable shoes and clothing that can be layered to accommodate changing climates.

- Leave expensive electronics and valuable jewelry at home.

2. Stay healthy. Getting sick when traveling in other countries will be time-consuming and take the fun out of the adventure, so take care of your health before you leave and when you travel. When you're traveling, follow these general health tips:

- Get plenty of sleep, especially if you're often changing time zones.

- Avoid drinking too much alcohol, this will dehydrate you and can lead to poor decisions.

- Drink plenty of purified water. Unless you've checked ahead of time, the tap water at your destination may not be as clean and safe to drink as your local water at home.

- Eat a somewhat balanced diet. In unfamiliar countries, it can be tempting to eat an unhealthy diet (or even one comprised of junk food). Keep yourself healthy by eating regular, balanced meals.

- Wash your hands often.

3. Invest in a global cell phone. Most domestic cell phones (i.e. the phone you currently use) will build up exorbitant fees if you use them internationally. You can be a world traveler and still stay

in touch with family and friends by purchasing a universal cell phone that will work all over the world.

- Before you look into an international cell phone, check with your current cell provider—they may be able to add an international calling plan for an additional monthly charge.

- Depending on the number of countries you'll be traveling in, and the duration of your stay(s), it may be more practical to rent an international phone in each country, rather than buying a single phone for your entire trip.

- International cell phones sometimes require that you buy separate SIM cards or recharge it with more minutes, but will keep you in constant contact with familiar people.

4. Prevent yourself from getting too homesick. A great way to do this is by keeping in touch with the people you miss the most. Whether through a phone call, a Skype or FaceTime session, or sending a postcard, communicating with your friends and loved ones will help bridge the distance and keep you from feeling homesick.

How to Travel to South America

South America is a large continent filled with diverse cultures and dazzling natural wonders. With so much to see, the hardest part about traveling there might just be deciding where to go. Before you leave, do your homework so you're prepared and have your major travel arrangements taken care of. Once you're there, make the most of the trip by soaking up the local sights and culture. Use a little common sense while you're abroad, and you'll have a safe and unforgettable adventure.

Part 1. Choosing the Vacation that Fits your Style

1. Choose your destination. South America is a large continent with many countries. Locations like Brazil, Argentina, Chile and Uruguay are well-developed and easy to navigate. Other countries, like Bolivia, Peru, Colombia, and Ecuador are a little less visited by tourists, but have their own treasures to offer. Popular destinations include:

- Brazil, with its lively cities like Rio de Janeiro.

- The Ancient Inca city Machu Picchu (Peru).

- The Amazon Jungle (Brazil, Peru, Columbia).

- Patagonia (Argentina and Chile).

- The Andes mountains (Venezuela, Colombia, Ecuador, Peru, Bolivia, Argentina and Chile).

- The Atacama Desert (Chile).

- The Galapagos Islands off the coast of Ecuador.

2. Pick the best season for your trip. Go in the spring or fall if you want to see some natural sights like the glaciers in the mountains. October or November is also a great time to see the rain forests. December to March, on the other hand, is the best time for festivals like Carnival.

- Keep in mind that seasons in the Northern and Southern hemispheres always run opposite to each other.

3. Choose your accommodations. Decide if you want to stay in hotels, hostels, or homestays. Hotels can offer standardized, world-class experiences, while hostels will give you a chance to interact with travelers from around the world at affordable rates. If you rent a homestay (through Airbnb, for instance), you get to vacation in a local's house for an authentic experience.

- Any of these types of accommodations can be found throughout South America. However, well-developed areas in Brazil, Argentina, Chile, and Uruguay will have the largest selection of hotels.

- Areas like Bolivia, Peru, Colombia and Ecuador will be cheaper, but have fewer options for accommodations.

- Choose accommodations that are highly rated on travel sites to ensure the best experience.

4. Go for an all-inclusive package to have accommodation plans taken care of. Talk to a travel agent or book a package online. Pre-packaged resorts can take care of flight and accommodation

arrangements for you. They may also include preset destination tours. These can be relatively expensive, however.

5. Join a destination tour for a sightseeing guide. You can purchase tickets to join tours at most popular tourist destinations. If you're an independent spirit, you might prefer to make your way on your own. If not, a tour guide can help arrange entry to attractions in your destination country.

6. Make continental travel arrangements. When you're in South America, take advantage of the local buses if you want to travel between cities. They're the most common transportation method on the continent. Trains are available in many areas as well. The train services in areas like Brazil have convenient websites so you can check the timetables and fare information.

- Road conditions can be unpredictable in parts of South America, outside of major cities. Renting a car will not be the most convenient option for getting around, unless you are planning to use it only for a short time in a city.

Part 2. Preparing for your Journey

1. Get your passport and visa. You'll need the passport to make international travel, and most countries in South America will require a visa for entry. You can get in touch with the state department in your home country for details on making arrangements. You can also work with a travel agent who can make the arrangements for you.

- Apply for these well ahead of your travel dates. It can take several months for a passport application to go through. Plan on a few weeks for visa processing.

- You may be required to get some vaccines before traveling. Even if they're not required, get them if your state department recommends them.

2. Learn some basics of the language. Get a phrasebook, study with an app, or read travel-oriented language sites so you won't feel lost when abroad. Most countries in South America use Spanish as the official language, but in Brazil Portuguese is the main language. Learn enough at least for the basics, like:

- Hello

- Please and thank you

- My name is...

- I need help

- Do you speak English?

- Where is...

- How much is this?

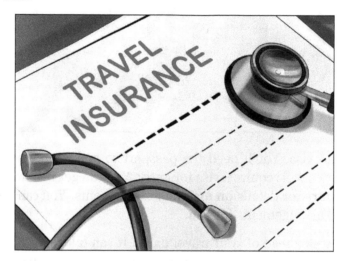

3. Purchase travel insurance. Buy at least minimum coverage so that you can see a doctor when traveling if you get sick or injured--you can't guarantee that your home insurance will apply abroad. Travel insurance is usually quite inexpensive, and you can work through a travel agency to make the application process quick and easy.

4. Pack clothing for a variety of climates. Bring both cool and warm weather clothing, no matter the season you're traveling during. Weather in South America can vary greatly depending on where you go. Deserts can be hot during the day, but become quite cold at night, for instance.

- For instance, you might want to pack some long pants and a short sleeve shirt for mild weather. Pack a light jacket in case the temperature drops.

5. Get the currencies you need. Exchange currency when you're in the airport or as soon as you get to your first destination. Each country in South America uses its own currency, so you might need to be prepared with several kinds, or else exchange several times.

- You can check with a bank or currency exchange in your home country before you go, if you prefer. However, you won't get the most-up to date currency exchange rates when you travel (though this may or may not work to your advantage).

6. Set travel alerts for your finances. Let your bank and credit card company know that you will be traveling abroad. That way, you won't end up having your card frozen while in South America.

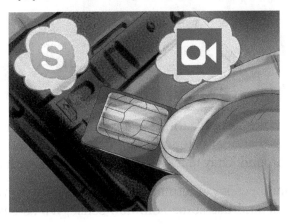

7. Get an international cell phone. If you already have a global phone or device that allows you to

use an international SIM card, you're set. Otherwise, you could ask your service provider if there are options allowing you to use your phone while traveling abroad.

- There are free options for communicating with back home, too. For instance, you can try Skype or Facetime.

Part 3. Staying Safe While Traveling

1. Check your state department's website for travel information. Look up the destination(s) you are traveling to and see if there is any information you need to know. This could include things like customs in the area, access to medical care if needed, safety concerns for travelers, etc.

2. Try to blend in. Keep a low profile by wearing plain clothes, and leaving jewelry, expensive watches, etc. at home. Stick to areas that cater to tourists unless you have a guide or know your way around. Don't flash wads of money around. Only take out a small amount of cash at a time.

- South America sometimes is sometimes said to be unsafe for travelers. In reality, if you avoid traveling alone and use some common sense, it's as easy to travel there as anywhere.

3. Check in with your embassy. When you arrive in your destination country, go to or call your nation's nearest embassy. Let them know you have arrived, and what your travel plans are. That way, they can keep tabs on you and help you out if you get into any trouble.

4. Keep in touch with your hotel's concierge. Let them know about your travel plans, too, and ask them any questions about getting around. They're not only a way to get tips on great restaurants and attractions--they can also advise you on how to stay safe and have a great trip in South America.

- For instance, ask the concierge questions like "Can you recommend an English-speaking tour guide?" or "Is there a bank nearby where I can withdraw cash, instead of using an ATM on the street?"

How to Travel to Canada

Canada is a fabulous travel destination. Before you travel, get any required travel documents, like your passport or travel visa. Review online to determine if you need a visa or just a passport to enter. Book your flight or bus ride, reserve hotels, and explore places like Toronto, Quebec, and the national parks in Canada. With some planning and research, you can easily book your dream vacation.

Part 1. Obtaining your Travel Documents

1. Figure out if you need a travel visa based on your home country. Most countries are able to travel to Canada simply with a passport, such as the United States, but there are some exceptions, like China and Cuba. To find out if you need a visa, go to the Canadian Government's website and answer citizenship questions appropriately.

- The questions will ask whether you are a dual citizen of Canada, permanent resident, refugee, stateless individual, former resident of Canada, or none of the above.

2. Review the visa or passport information based on your home country. The website will provide further instructions on how to apply for a travel visa or how to see if your citizenship is still valid. If you selected "None of the above," select the 3 letter code of that matches your passport and click "Go." The next page will explain whether you can visit Canada with just a passport or if a visa is required.

- The 3 letter code will correspond with your country of citizenship. For example, USA is for the United States of America and ARE is for the United Arab Emirates.

- Some countries have multiple codes depending on regions, so make sure your code matches exactly as it reads on the passport. For instance, there are 6 codes for the United Kingdom.

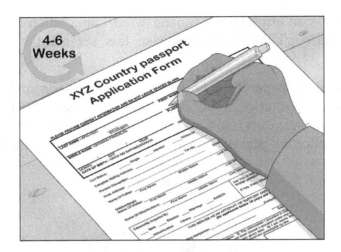

3. Obtain a passport from your country of citizenship if you don't have one. You need a passport to enter Canada, but every country handles their citizenship slightly different. Visit your government's website and go to the "Passport" page to review specifics. Generally, you must be a citizen in good standing, apply in person with your biographic documents, provide a passport photo, pay the application fee, and get accepted.

- Apply for your passport as early as you can. They typically take 4-6 weeks to obtain.

- Some countries offer online applications. Check online to see if this is an option for your country, if you prefer.

- If you hold dual citizenship with Canada and another country, ensure your passport is valid.

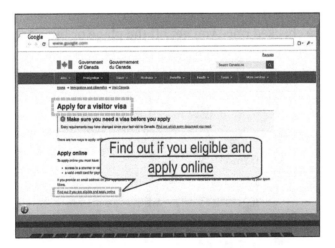

4. Apply for a Canadian tourist visa if you need it to enter Canada. In addition to your passport, you may need a visa to enter Canada. If you do, you can easily apply for a visa online. Go to https://www.canada.ca/en/immigration-refugees-citizenship/services/visit-canada/apply-visitor-visa.html to get started. Complete the application with information like your biographical details and citizen status, pay your application fee online, and submit your application. Then, submit any required documents or forms. You may be instructed to mail in additional documents.

- Before you apply, visit https://www.canada.ca/en/immigration-refugees-citizenship/services/visit-canada/eligibility.html?lnktrk=visa_less_six_months to review the eligibility requirements.

- You may also apply on paper if you prefer. For instructions on applying, visit http://www.cic.gc.ca/english/information/applications/visa.asp?_ga=2.126454542.2001609413.1521752144-1927941775.1519337130#applyonpaper, select your country of citizenship, and download the application package. Then, follow the outlined instructions.

5. Bring your travel documents with you when you go to Canada. No matter your transportation method, you must bring your documents with you to enter Canada.

- If you are driving to Canada, show your travel documents when you cross the border.

- If you are taking a plane, train, or bus to Canada, you must have your travel documents to board. They will be checked once you get off the plane or bus as well.

Part 2. Planning your Accommodations

1. Set a budget to determine how much you can spend on your trip. Consider your total costs of your trip, including travel, lodging, transportation, food and drinks, excursions, and shopping. It is also helpful to set aside some funds in case of an emergency. Your budget will depend on

your specific travel desires and income, though you can surely travel to Canada if you are on a budget.

- Set your travel budget for a number like $500 (£353.28) or more, for example.

2. Decide on your travel dates. Canada is a popular destination during all seasons. You can visit for a few days or a few weeks, depending on your schedule and travel desires. Select your dates of travel so you can book your travel accommodations.

- If you enjoy winter sports like skiing or snowboarding, traveling to Canada in the winter is a great idea to take advantage of the snow.

- If you enjoy sightseeing and city travel, go during the spring or summer.

- To explore Canada's wilderness, go during any season and view the majestic mountains, rivers, and lakes.

- Be sure to check the length of your visa if you have one, and don't stay past the time outlined to avoid immigration issues.

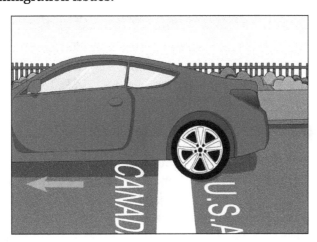

3. Drive to Canada if you live close to the border in the United States. Locate your closest border checkpoint online, and show your travel documents when you arrive. In addition, briefly interview with a Canadian border officer when you arrive.

- The officer will ask you details like the length of your trip, where you are going, and what items you have with you. They may ask to inspect your car as well.

4. Take a bus or train to Canada if you live in the United States. There are many coach bus and train companies companies that offer rides to Canada from the United States. Go online and search for "Bus to Canada" or "Train to Canada" and review options from companies, like Greyhound or Amtrak.

- In addition, you can take trains or buses to get around Canada once you are inside the country. Canada's train service is called Via Rail.

5. Fly to Canada if you live abroad or want to cut down on travel time. If you live outside of the United States, your best bet for traveling to Canada is taking an airplane. To find flights, search "Flights to Canada" review the travel options based on your intended dates. Insert your desired airports and select your arriving and departing dates.

- To get the best rates, search for and book your flights 1-3 months in advance.

- If you'd like a shorter trip to Canada, consider flying from the United States. Planes take a fraction of the time it can take via ground transportation.

6. Book your lodging in advance. Lodging options include hotels, hostels, cabins, or campgrounds. Search something like "Places to stay in Toronto" or "Hotels in Niagara Falls" to find options online. Hotels are great to accommodate your entire family, and hostels are an affordable option for travelers looking to share social experiences. If you enjoy the outdoors, consider camping or renting a cabin.

- Book your lodging at least 2 weeks to 1 month before your trip

- Alternatively, if you have friends or family in Canada, you can stay with them to save on travel costs.

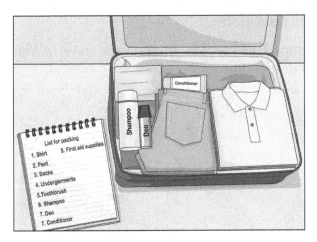

7. Draft a packing list before you go. To help you pack for your trip, write down a packing list so you don't forget anything. Create different headings for clothing, toiletries, technology, and travel documents. Base your list around the length of your trip. Use your packing list as you prepare your luggage so you are well organized and ready for to go.

- For example, if you are traveling for 1 week, bring 7 shirts, 7 pants, and extra socks and underwear. You may want to pack in many layers and bring some back-up clothing, just in case.

- Pack toiletries like your toothbrush, toothpaste, shampoo, conditioner, and deodorant.

- Don't forget any required medication and first aid supplies.

- When you pack your clothing, go with versatile options. For example, you can wear a maxi dress during day trips as well as dress it up with heels and jewelry for a night out.

Part 3. Planning your Travel Itinerary

1. Research popular destinations and activities to make a rough itinerary. Go online and search for things like "Things to do in Canada." There are countless travel guide websites to assist you in planning your trip. Canada has 12 provinces or territories, so there is plenty to see throughout this vast country.

- You can do things like visit historic monuments, explore popular cities like Montreal and Toronto, or go hiking and fishing.

- You can also visit https://us-keepexploring.canada.travel/#WhereToGo and browse activities based on your destination.

2. Go see Niagara Falls in Ontario to explore a natural wonder. Niagara Falls is an epic collection of waterfalls that span between Ontario and New York along the Niagara river. It is one of the most popular destinations in Canada, and you can visit the falls during all 4 seasons.

- There is also tons of shopping, restaurant, and lodging in Niagara falls.

- You can take a Maid of the Mist boat tour to see the falls up close and personal. Be sure to wear your poncho.

3. See the Northern Lights in autumn and winter for a dazzling sight. Aurora borealis is a mysterious, gorgeous natural occurrence bringing people to Canada from all across the globe. To see this stunning light display, travel to Canada's northwest territories, like Newfoundland or Labrador. You have a greater chance of seeing the Northern Lights the closer you venture to the North Pole.

- You can see the Northern Lights from many of Canada's territories and national parks. It is visible all throughout Canada, though the best viewing conditions are in northern Canada.

- Aurora borealis is visible in the northwest territories nearly 240 nights of the year.

- You can also hire a guide to help you with travel, transportation, and viewing locations.

4. Visit National Parks in Canada if you enjoy outdoor activities. The national parks protect Canada's gorgeous natural landscapes for citizens and visitors to explore and appreciate. Canada has 39 natural regions to explore, consisting of mountains, plains, forests, lakes, tundras, and glaciers. To find a national park in the territory you want to visit, go to https://www.pc.gc.ca/en/pn-np/recherche-parcs-parks-search.

- Visit popular national parks like Banff and Glacier, to name a few.

- This is a great option if you like hiking, climbing, cycling, fishing, or camping.

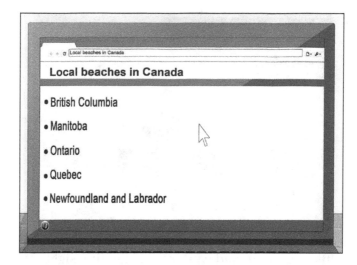

5. Travel to one of Canada's coasts if you want to check out the beaches. Canada may be known for its mountains and winter sports, but there are miles and miles of coastal beaches you can explore. Visit in the summer months when temperatures are the warmest if you want to swim. You can swim in either the Pacific or Atlantic ocean, as well as many of the Great Lakes and the Hudson Bay. There are beaches lining British Columbia, Manitoba, Ontario, Quebec, Newfoundland, and Nova Scotia.

- Search online for local beaches and attractions in these areas.

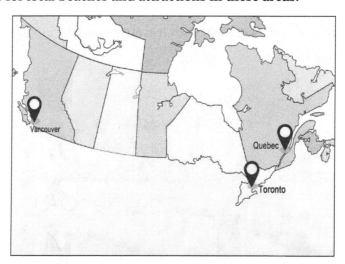

6. Explore cities like Toronto, Quebec, and Vancouver if you like history. If you prefer city adventures, Canada has many awesome options to choose from. Each city has its own extensive list of things to do, though be sure to visit art and history museums and explore popular historic sites. You can do some shopping and eat Canadian food staples like poutine.

- If you want to go to Toronto, explore things like the Hockey Hall of Fame, the Toronto Zoo, and the CN Tower.

- For Quebec visitors, visit the battlefields park, Notre Dame de Quebec Basilica, and Palace Royale. It is also helpful to brush up on your French.

- If traveling to Vancouver, check out places like Granville Island, VanDusen Botanical Garden, and the University of British Columbia Museum of Anthropology.

7. Climb the CN Tower for a stunning view if you like visiting cities. The CN Tower is a famous observation tower in downtown Toronto. Built in 1976, it consists of 1,776 steps and 144 flights of stairs. At one point, it held the record for the tallest building and freestanding structure. You can climb the CN tower in about 30-40 minutes. When you reach the top, you get to see a spectacular view of downtown Toronto.

- Do this if you enjoy visiting cities and learning about interesting architecture.

8. Check out the Notre Dame Basilica Cathedral if you are a history buff. Notre Dame in Quebec was the first cathedral build in North America, and it dates back to 1647. It is the grave site of 4 governers of New France, and there is various artwork and archives on display as well. The structure is intricately tied to the history and development of Quebec, Canada, and North America, so if you enjoy history, you can learn a lot if you visit.

- This is a World Heritage Site located in Old Montreal.

9. Visit Drumheller if you want to see the dinosaur capital of the world. Drumheller is a small town in Alberta known for its prestigious collection of dinosaur and fossil exhibits. It is located in the heart of the Canadian Badlands, and you can trek many hiking trails and view canyons and lookouts as well.

- Other things to do in Drumheller include taking a horseback tour through the Badlands and exploring the Atlas Coal Mine.

How to Visit the United States

Whether you're visiting family or vacationing in the United States, you'll need to meet entry requirements for your country of origin. If you're a citizen of a country that participates in the Visa Waiver Program (VWP), you'll just need to fill out an ESTA (Electronic System for Travel Authorization) application. If your country isn't eligible, you'll need to apply for a visitor visa, which can take several months. Upon arrival, present your passport and, if necessary, your visa. Fill out a customs declaration form, clear customs, then enjoy a wonderful trip.

Method 1. Visiting the US from a VWP Country

1. Use the US State Department's visa wizard to find your requirements. Enter your country of origin and purpose of travel into the visa wizard, then click "Find a Visa." The tool will let you know

if your country participates in the VWP or if you need to apply for a visitor visa. As of December 2017, citizens of 38 countries are eligible to travel to the US under the VWP.

- Find the visa wizard here: https://travel.state.gov/content/travel/en/us-visas/visa-information-resources/wizard.html.

- Visitors traveling to the US under the VWP can stay without a visa for up to 90 days.

2. Ensure you have a valid e-passport. In order to enter the US under the VWP, you must have an e-passport, which is a passport that contains an electronic chip. E-passports have a unique symbol on the front cover. It looks like a circle inscribed within a rectangle.

- You'll need your passport to fill out an ESTA (Electronic System for Travel Authorization) application and to enter the US.

- For some countries, your passport must be valid for 6 months beyond the duration of your trip. However, several dozen countries are exempt from the 6 month rule. If you're exempt, your passport only needs to be valid during the length of your visit.

3. Submit an ESTA application at least 72 hours before your trip. The US Customs and Border Protection recommends that visitors apply for ESTA at least 72 hours before travel, but you can apply any time before your visit. Authorization is valid for 2 years, and you can make multiple trips

during that time. You'll need to enter your passport, contact, and employment information, and pay a $14 (USD) application fee.

- Usually, applicants receive a response within seconds of submitting an ESTA form. Once you're authorized you'll just need to present your passport and go through customs when you arrive in the US.

- Complete your ESTA application here: https://esta.cbp.dhs.gov/esta/esta.html.

Method 2. Applying for a Visitor's Visa

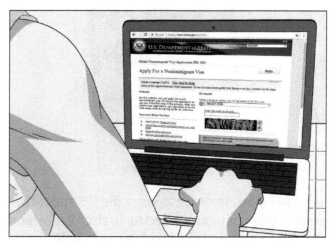

1. Begin the visa application process as soon as possible. In some countries, it can take at least 6 months to complete the visa application process. Fill out the online application and schedule your interview as far in advance as possible.

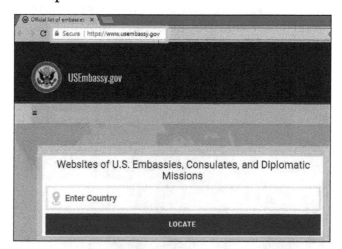

2. Locate your US embassy or consulate and visit its website. Your nearby US embassy or consulate website includes specific application instructions for your country. You'll need to identify your embassy or consulate location on your application, and you'll need to schedule an interview on its website.

- Locate the nearest US embassy or consulate here: https://www.usembassy.gov.

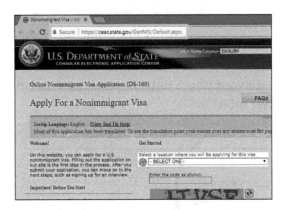

3. Submit Form DS-160 online. Head to the visa application form on the US Department of State website, then select your embassy to start the application. You'll need your passport, information about your purpose of travel, itinerary, employment information, and any other documents specified on your embassy or consulate's website.

- Begin your visa application here: https://ceac.state.gov/genniv.

- After submitting your application, you'll receive a visa application confirmation page. Print this confirmation and bring it with you to the interview.

4. Pay the visa application fee. Fees vary by country of origin, but are usually around $160 (USD). Depending on your country, you'll either pay the fee at an authorized bank before your interview or at the interview itself. If you pay in advance, bring your receipt of payment to the interview.

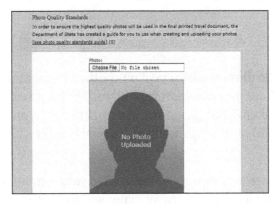

5. Upload a photograph that meets visa requirements with Form DS-160. When you submit Form

DS-160, you'll need to upload a color photo taken within the last 6 months. Similar to a passport photo, the visa photo needs to meet a variety of requirements, so it's best to have a professional visa photo service take it.

- If there's a problem with your photo upload, you'll have to bring a printed copy that meets all requirements to your interview.

6. Schedule an interview with your embassy or consulate. Schedule your interview on the website of the nearest embassy or consulate. In some countries, you might have to wait up to 4 months for an interview. When you schedule the interview, you'll have an option to check wait times for your embassy or consulate.

7. Bring your passport, application confirmation, and other required documents to the interview. A foreign service officer will ask you questions about your trip and establish that you're legally eligible to enter the US. Give them your passport, your printed visa application confirmation page, payment receipt (if applicable), and documents that show you'll be able to return to your country of origin.

- A letter from your current employer confirming your employment and bank statements can help prove that you can afford travel expenses and return to your country. Documents confirming your purpose of travel, such as a wedding invitation, will also be helpful.

- Your passport will be returned by mail or courier service after your application is processed.

- You'll also be digitally fingerprinted during your interview.

8. Allow at least 60 days for processing and shipping. Some applications require additional processing, which can take up to 60 days. You'll find out if this is the case during your interview. Even if your application doesn't require additional processing, it could still take several weeks for you to receive your visa and passport by mail or courier service.

Method 3. Planning your Trip to the US

1. Choose a destination that suits your interests. The US is a vast country with thousands of miles of coastline, stunning geological features, quaint towns, and bustling cities. If you don't have a specific reason to visit, like a wedding or graduation, learn about American attractions and decide what to include in your itinerary. Start by looking up destinations organized by regions, states, and cities on https://www.visittheusa.com/.

- You could shop, catch a Broadway show, and get a bird's eye view from the top of the Empire State Building in New York City. Since the Northeast is densely populated, you could easily take day trips from New York to Boston, Philadelphia, or Washington, DC. If you're more interested in nature's wonder, hike the Grand Canyon or hit the slopes in Colorado. If you're a beach bum, head to California, the Gulf of Mexico, or the Atlantic Coast's Gulf Stream waters.

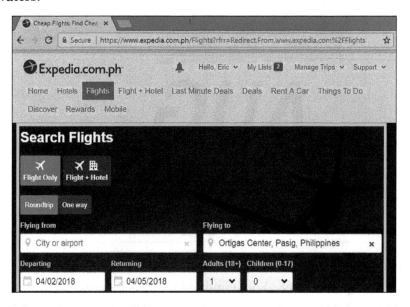

2. Book travel arrangements. If you haven't already, purchase your plane ticket or make other travel accommodations. Depending on your point of departure, you'll likely spend a lot of time on a plane. Pack a neck pillow, a good book, podcasts, music, and other sources of entertainment. Do your best to pass the time, and walk around and stretch regularly to avoid back or joint pain.

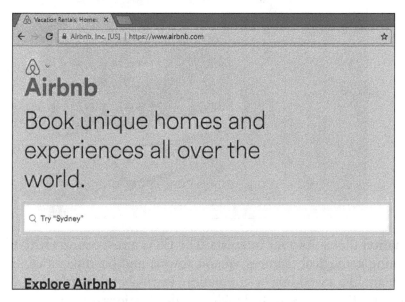

3. Book a hotel or other accommodations, if necessary. If you're not staying with relatives, arrange for a place to stay in advance of your trip. Shop for hotel room deals online or through your travel agent. You could also explore alternative options, such as an Airbnb vacation rental.

4. Consider purchasing medical insurance. Medical treatment in the US is expensive if you're uninsured, and American healthcare can seem truly foreign if you're used to a universal insurance system. Taking out a medical insurance policy for travelers could save you thousands in the event of an emergency.

- For example, suppose you break your ankle while skiing in Denver, Colorado. Without insurance, expect to pay at least $6,500 (USD).

5. Exchange currency and learn about American pricing. Call your bank to ensure your credit cards function internationally, and exchange currency so you have cash just in case. For the best rate, exchange currency at your bank before your trip. When shopping or dining, keep in mind the listed price doesn't include sales tax, which is usually around 7 percent.

- Additionally, it's customary to tip your server 15 to 20 percent at restaurants. In most states, servers make $2 to $3 per hour and depend on tips to make a living.

Method 4. Arriving in the US

1. Present your passport, visa, or other required documents upon arrival. Nearly all foreign

nationals must present a valid passport upon arriving in the US. If your country of origin does not participate in the VWP, you'll also need to present your visa. Procedures are slightly different for citizens of Canada, Bermuda, and Mexico.

- If you're a Canadian citizen, you don't need to apply for ESTA. Canadian citizens traveling by land can present a valid passport or enhanced driver's license (a type of secure government-issued ID). Canadian citizens traveling by air must present a passport.

- Bermudian citizens do not need to apply for ESTA and only need to provide a valid passport.

- If you're a Mexican citizen, you can enter the United States with a valid passport along with a visitor visa or a Border Crossing Card. Apply for a Border Crossing Card at your nearby US embassy or consulate. It's usually valid 10 years after issuance.

2. Go through customs screening. Your passport, ESTA, visa, and other documentation don't guarantee entry into the US. Upon arrival, a customs agent will ask you about your purpose of travel and other questions in order to verify your eligibility to enter the US.

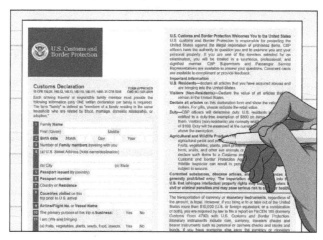

3. Complete a customs declaration form. Whether you're a US citizen or foreign national, you must complete a declarations form. This provides information about who you are, why you're traveling, and what you're bringing into the country.

4. Depart the US by your admitted-until or D/S date. When you clear customs, the officer will issue either an admission stamp or Form I-94 with an admitted until date or a Duration of Stay (D/S) date. You must depart the US by this date. Failure to do so could render you ineligible for future entry into the US.

How to Travel to Germany

Germany is a country that lies within the very centre of Europe, as everyone knows. When you think of Germany, you probably think of cars, beer, sausages and Rammstein (a German industrial metal band that are well known around the world). Here's how you go there.

Steps

1. Read about Germany in order to determine which areas and activities are of most interest to you. You might wish to spend time visiting car factories in the industrial city of Munich. Or perhaps you want to travel to the castles in the lakes region. Many libraries offer excellent travel books, or you could pick one up fairly cheaply at a bookstore. It's also possible to download travel books to a smart phone, and carry all that information with you as you travel.

2. Prepare your travel documents ahead of time by researching whether you need a passport or a visa for travel from your country. Leave yourself plenty of time to get your documents up to date. If you live in Europe, you may benefit from relaxed requirements in this regard, Germany being part of the Schengen Area. This is a group of countries in Europe that have agreed to let citizens of other nearby countries into their territory with minimal or no border controls. Check for the latest configuration of the Schengen Area if you think you live in a country which is part of this reciprocal agreement.

3. Learn some German. Try the colorful DuoLingo, an app available for mobile devices, or for more intensive language listening practice, use something LingQ.com, a web based service which makes it easy to teach yourself a variety of languages. You will need to communicate with other people in Germany, and knowing a little of the language will help. However, you may also find that English is widely spoken. At the very least, when you choose a travel book, look for one with a bit of a glossary of basic terms, or buy a phrase book. It is also worth learning something about German etiquette and tipping, which again, will be covered in your tourbook.

4. Decide how you are going to travel, whether by plane, by ship, by car, or by train. Book your tickets, or make your reservations, in advance. Online services are available to help.

5. Decide where you want to go and book accommodation there. Hotels are available, or you might want to try a service where you can rent space in someone's home, or rent an entire apartment.

6. Convert a small amount of money into Euros (if you don't already have some) and take them with you so you will have cash when you arrive. Watch the exchange rate as you plan your trip, and you will have a pretty good idea of how many Euros your currency is going to buy you. Take a couple of credit cards with you, but don't plan on using those for cash advances. Instead, get cash while there, by use of your ATM card at banks. Take at least two different ATM cards in case you lose one, or in case a bank machine grabs or mangles one. Note that the German post office has offered no fee ATM withdrawals. Check to see if this is still the case when you travel, as the post office may be your best deal for ATM withdrawals.

7. Buy a good money belt and use it for your passport, cards, and cash. Pickpocketing is a major problem in the busier tourist areas.

8. Pack what you need for the trip. Be sure to bring a camera, that you have practiced with ahead of time.

9. Once the day comes, board the plane (or a train if you booked a train ticket) and go to Germany. Take care not to leave your luggage behind on any part of the journey, or you're up the creek without a paddle.

10. Enjoy your trip.

How to Move to Switzerland

Do you desire to move to the neutral country Switzerland? Switzerland is a country with four languages, extensive history, and plenty to discover. While a beautiful country, Switzerland is notorious as a difficult country to move to, and there are many things to consider before moving.

Part 1. Making your Decision

1. Determine your motivations for moving. Are you trying to get a better job? To get a better life-style? To get a better education? To escape from unhappiness at home? Understand your motives, and evaluate alternatives to see whether moving to Switzerland is the best option.

2. Write down all the reasons you want to move to Switzerland. For example:

- Switzerland is famous for its beautiful mountains. The temperate climate in Switzerland, varying from glacial mountaintops to pleasant Mediterranean climate at the southern tip. Summers tend to be warm and humid, with periodic rainfall, so they are ideal for pastures and grazing.

- Switzerland has one of the most stable economies in the world. The Swiss franc remains one of the world's strongest currencies with the lowest inflation rate.

- Switzerland remains very open to foreigners and has a diverse population. Resident foreigners and temporary foreign workers make up about 22% of the population.

- Religious freedom: Switzerland has no official state religion. Christianity is the predominant religion of Switzerland, divided between the Catholic Church (41.8% of the population) and various Protestant denominations (35.3%). Islam (4.3%) and Eastern Orthodoxy (1.8%) are sizable minority religions. Greeley (2003) found that 27% of Swiss are atheists.

- Switzerland is particularly suited for skiing, snowboarding and mountaineering, which are enjoyed by both locals and tourists.

3. Research Switzerland. Check out books from your local library or bookstore, search the internet, ask around people who have been to Switzerland or know about the country. Be familiar with the country's cultures, traditions, laws, religions, cost of living, climate, language, transportation, etc.

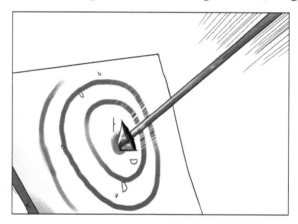

4. Make your decision. Moving to another country is a big decision in your life, so be sure to take your time and consult with your friends and loved ones. You must be absolutely convinced that moving to Switzerland is better than staying where you are, and that it is the best country for you to move to.

Part 2. Making It Happen

1. Get your documentation in order. A passport is a must for Americans. You will probably require a passport to travel by plane to Switzerland wherever you travel from if you live in Europe already,

a passport may not be required, you may be able to cross the border from another European country unchallenged. Remember Switzerland is not part of the European Union. Get all required legal documents, such as passports, visa and work permits. This is essential, or you cannot gain entry into Switzerland. Visit the Federal Office of Immigration, Integration and Emigration if it helps, for all questions pertaining to visas and regulations. It is very easy to follow and has detailed information in four languages.

2. Secure a job, preferably from a large international company based in Switzerland. They will typically help you get a work permit. There are many internet resources that can help you find a job in Switzerland. Excellent job search tool, with many international positions including Switzerland.</ref> Most Swiss employers are great employers, and many of them are even willing to hire someone with the technical skills they need regardless of language proficiency. (The Swiss languages are German, French, and Italian, each spoken primarily in areas of the Switzerland neighboring the respective countries.) If you work for a company in the US that has an office in Switzerland, you may be able to apply for a transfer. If not, consider looking for such company.

- Know that highly qualified specialists and top executives are awarded work and residence permits, in lieu of the above step. If that applies to you, you may apply for such permit. Be aware that this type of permit is extremely hard to obtain and even harder to get renewed.

- Take advantage of the three month rule: you are allowed to stay in the country legally for up to three months. Ensure that you are entitled to work during the three months. Take small jobs such as babysitting or English teachers, while looking for permanent work during the three month period. If you fail to find permanent work, don't be discouraged, but simply try again. When the three month period is up, leave the country for a while, then return for another three month visit to resume the job search.

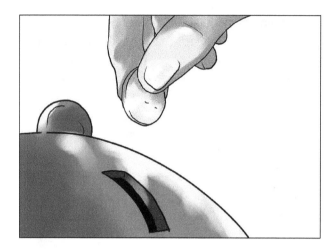

3. Establish a budget. Switzerland is the wealthiest country in the world, with an average per-capita income about £28,000 a year, and is one of the most expensive country to live in. If this does not deter you, you need to bring enough money to get a good start once you arrive, and be very conservative with spending every penny.

4. Book your transportation to Switzerland. For example:

- From Britain: Flying is by far the easiest, cheapest, and most convenient way to get from Britain to Switzerland. Travelling by train is comfortable and scenic, but is more expensive and takes more than a day. Trains and buses are worth considering if you are interested in visiting other parts of Europe during the trip.

- From North America: Several airlines fly direct from North America to Zürich; many other airlines offer flights to Zürich via other major European cities.

- From Australia and New Zealand: Flying is the cheapest and easiest option. Fares vary significantly with the season: low season runs from mid-January to the end of February and during October and November; high season runs from mid-May to the end of August and from December to mid-January; the rest of the year is considered "shoulder season". So plan to travel during low season if possible. Find the best deal. Travel agents often offer better deals than buying direct from airlines.

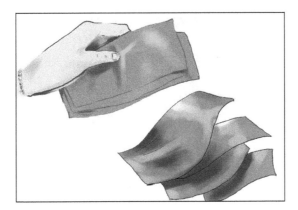

5. Convert your currency into Swiss francs. Note that the symbol for the Swiss franc is CHF, which stands for Confoederatio Helvetica Franc; the official name of Switzerland is Confoederatio Helvetica, or Swiss Confederation. Remember, the more money you bring, the better start that you will get in Switzerland. The rate of currency conversion may fluctuate, so keep a look out on the foreign exchange market, as you may be able to get a little bit extra money (especially if you are converting a lot of money).

6. Import your belongings. For example:

- Pets: You may freely import cats and dogs without a permit. Obtain a rabies vaccination certificate from a veterinarian. The certificate must be written in German, French, Italian, or English can contain name and address of animal owner, description of the animal (breed, sex, age, color), confirmation that the animal was submitted to a veterinary examination prior to vaccination and found in good health, date of rabies vaccination, type of vaccine used, name of manufacturer and batch number, & signature of the veterinarian. Certificates in other languages are accepted if accompanied by a legal translation. Guinea pigs, hamsters, rats, mice, aquarium fish, and canaries can be imported without a veterinary certificate. Domestic animals and dangerous animals require import permits from the Federal Veterinary Office.

- Weapons: Obtain authorization from your place of origin to import weapons.

- Cars: You must pay import duty (consisting of customs duties based on weight of the vehicle and engine capacity; 4% consumption tax; 7.5% Value added tax; and 15-Fr for the report) to import a car that you owned for less than six months. Contact is the customs authority for full details. Cars you owned for more than six months are exempt from import duty and will simply require filling out a clearance request form. Also consider selling your cars and buying a car in Switzerland, or use a bike or public transportation.

7. Pack your luggage. Big items can be imported separately, so pack only what you can fit into a bag, such as books, clothes, personal care items and money.

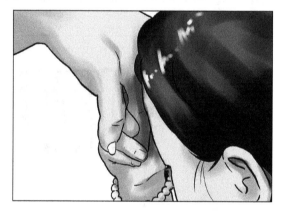

8. Say goodbye to loved ones who will not accompanying you on the move. This is likely to be very emotional, so remember to bring tissues. Hug each other and tell them you love them, and invite them to come visit any time they want. Promise to keep in regular touch, and do so.

9. Board your mode of transport, and go to Switzerland. Relax on the trip, and feel excited about starting a new life, in a new country. Do not worry too much about friends or family, as they will come and visit often, and you will make plenty of new friends.

Part 3. Living in Switzerland

1. Look for a house/apartment in Switzerland. Visiting the country will offer you an opportunity to find a place. Real estate agents can help you in the process; alternatively, you can read books and search the internet.

2. Have utilities installed, find a school for your children, etc. once you get there.

3. Meet new people everywhere you go: at work, in the library, at the gym, at school, or at your hobby club. Check out all the resources available to help you integrate into the community

- groups.yahoo.com/group/Expats-in-Switzerland/ - A discussion forum full of good advice about many practical issues], from moving to Switzerland to finding peanut butter and maple syrup. Here you can find a large list of more specific newsgroups and online communities for Switzerland.

- xpatxchange.ch/ - A one-stop shop for English speaking ex-pats in Switzerland, full of advice, businesses, addresses. It is perhaps more useful once you have arrived in Switzerland.

4. Obtain Swiss citizenship. Not only will becoming a Swiss citizen help you integrate into the country permanently, you will also be able to start your own businesses, no longer need to re-apply for residence permits when changing jobs, no longer need special permission before purchasing residential property, and be able to move freely within the country. There are two ways to become a Swiss citizen:

- By birth, if both parents are Swiss. Children born in Switzerland from non-Swiss parents do not automatically become Swiss.

- By naturalization. Make your request to the Aliens Police in the municipality of residence. From there, it will then be sent to the Federal Department of Justice and Police, who will give a principle authorization if you meet the following conditions:

  ○ You have resided in Switzerland for at least twelve years, three of which are within the five years prior to the request. Time spent in Switzerland between the ages of 10 and 20 years counts double.

  ○ You are integrated in the Swiss community.

  ○ You are accustomed to Swiss way of life and practices.

  ○ You comply with the Swiss legal system.

  ○ You do not compromise the internal or external security of Switzerland.

  ○ You are able to afford it. Since Switzerland is a federal country, authorization must then be obtained from the canton and the municipality, which may add further conditions and set the cost of acquiring citizenship before approving it. Some municipalities apply rather open policies, while others will go as far as granting nationality by means of a local population vote. Cost varies according to municipality and canton.

How to Visit the UK

The United Kingdom is an island nation made up of four different countries: England, Scotland, Wales, and Northern Ireland. It is a popular vacation destination with beautiful castles, countryside, and a rich history. If you're planning to visit the UK, make sure you have your passport and other legal documents before creating your itinerary and booking your trip.

Part 1. Reviewing the Legalities

1. Check if you need to apply for a visa. The UK has different tourism laws for people of other nationalities. For many European and English-speaking countries, you will not need a visa to visit in the UK short-term if you have a valid passport. Visit the official UK government website to determine if you need a visa: https://www.gov.uk/check-uk-visa.

- Citizens of the USA, Canada, or Australia may travel visa-free throughout the UK with a valid passport for up to 6 months.

- All citizens from European Union (EU) countries, Norway, Liechtenstein, Iceland, Switzerland, islands overseas associated with countries in the EU, and Japan do not need a visa to visit the UK if they are not staying longer than 6 months.

2. Apply for a passport at least 8 weeks in advance. You need a passport to visit the UK. Passports routinely take 6-8 weeks to receive unless you pay a fee to expedite the process.. Check your country's official government website for details on obtaining a passport.

- In the USA, you can apply for your passport in-person at any local post office

- When applying for a passport, you will need to bring proof of citizenship, a government-issued photo ID, and a color 2 x 2-inch photo printed on photo-quality paper that meets the requirements listed on your country's official government website.

- Passport fees must be paid at the time of the application. Check your government's official website for pricing and fees.

- Each person going on the trip will need to have their own passport, including children.

3. Review customs regulations for the UK. The UK has limitations on the amount of goods you can

bring if you are a citizen of a country outside of the EU. If you are a citizen of a country in the EU, you can bring an unlimited amount of most goods for personal use.

- Check the official UK government website for details about customs regulations:

Part 2. Creating your Itinerary

1. Budget all costs for the length of the trip. Decide how long your trip will be and write down all planned expenses to get an idea of the total cost. You can get a rough estimate of expenses by researching how much they are in the UK. If you underbudget the expenses, you may not be able to see and do all of the activities you want. Also, keep in mind that there may be hidden or unexpected fees that you should plan to cover. Expenses to budget for include:

- Air travel: plane ticket, check baggage fees, airport transfers, and any amenities you may purchase on the trip

- Lodging and meal accommodations: total hotel or hostel cost per night, meals (breakfast, lunch, and dinner) per person, and any snacking in between

- Transit during the trip: public transportation (buses, ferries, trains), car rental and gas, or taxis

- Sightseeing fees: entrance fees for tours and other activities; tickets for choirs, theatres, or festivals; and any souvenirs you may purchase

- And other necessary fees for passports, visas, travel insurance, and currency exchange

- It is wise to have an emergency cash fund as well in case of any miscellaneous or unplanned travel expenses.

2. Visit Belfast, Northern Ireland for Victorian scenery and historical attractions. Northern Ireland is known for its Victorian-era architecture, a style consistent between 1837 and 1901. In its capital city of Belfast, you can find pubs, buildings, and castles with this design, in addition to a botanical garden in the city center. There are several sightseeing tour buses that provide views around the city and down the Causeway Coast, a scenic route that overlooks Giant's Causeway, a vast natural rock formation that is millions of years old.

- Northern Ireland is one of many filming sets for the TV series Game of Thrones. You can buy touring tickets to visit the various places used in the series, including the Dark Hedges, an avenue of trees used to depict Kings Road, and the Ballintoy Harbor, used for panoramic shots of the Iron Islands.

- The Titanic Belfast is a tourist attraction that immerses you in the history of the Titanic ship, which was built in Belfast. The visitors center has rides, full-scale reconstructions, interactive features to explore the ship and the nearby ocean, and original artifacts.

3. Go to Scotland for historic castles and museums. The most popular cities in Scotland are Edinburgh, the country's capital, and Glasgow. Edinburgh is home to Edinburgh Castle, Georgian architecture reminiscent of the 1700s, and popular eateries, including whiskey tours. Glasgow

contains over 20 museums and art galleries, with renovated historic buildings around the city as pubs and restaurants and a vibrant music scene.

- Scotland has other gems as well, outside of city centers. Visit the Orkney Islands or Inner Hebrides in northern Scotland for a look at wildlife, or small St. Andrews for it world-renowned golf.

- If you're an adventurer, visit the mountainous Highlands for scenery and national park trails.

4. Explore England for the most iconic landmarks and diverse cities. England is the largest country in the UK and is home to many famous cities. Northern England has the vintage charm of Manchester and Liverpool, while the south side of the country contains notable Oxford and Birmingham. England's most visited city is London, the country's capital, with landmarks like Big Ben and London Bridge.

- London is filled with over 230 theaters, several eatery options from street food to world-renowned restaurants, and has guided tours to visit sights used as movie backdrops.

- Stonehenge, a prehistoric construction that dates back to the Stone Age, is also found in the south of England.

5. Visit Wales for a sociable, serene experience. Wales is known for its sleepy towns and scenic

landscapes. Wales is surrounded on 3 of its 4 sides by water, and its coast is lined with colorful architecture and friendly villages. Cardiff, the country's capital, is home to many castles and sociable locals.

- Visit Pembrokeshire, a coastal National Park, for golden beaches, rugged cliffs, and beautiful caves.

- Wales has several individual events and activities throughout the year along its coastline.

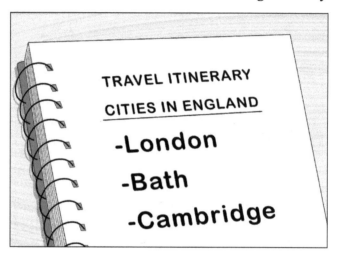

6. Create an itinerary of cities and attractions you want to visit. Write down the activities you are most eager to do and be mindful of the travel times between these items. Do not pack too many items into one trip; you may feel rushed to complete them all and not have enough time to enjoy the experience.

- Be mindful of the cost and make sure the attractions fit into your budget, including the transportation from one activity to the next.

Part 3. Scheduling your Trip

1. Decide how you will travel to the UK. There are several methods to get to the UK depending on where in the world you are located. The most popular option is air travel to one the UK's major

airports. If you are located in Europe, you may travel by ferry across the sea or by bus and train (via the Channel Tunnel).

- If you are in Europe, it is worth it to compare prices and comfort levels between the different travel options to get the lowest cost.

- If you are flying, you should search different airlines for their prices and to where they are flying in the UK.

- Book your travel arrangements in advance to take advantage of lower ticket prices.

2. Find lodging central to the areas you want to visit. Finding lodging accommodations close to the areas of the UK you want to visit will cut down on travel times and expenses. There are several different types of lodging available in the UK and they vary in price and amenities.

- Types of lodging include pubs and inns, bed-and-breakfasts (BnBs), hostels, traditional and boutique hotels, campsites, and housing offered on websites like Airbnb and HomeAway.

- Book your lodging and travel arrangements in advance. You will save yourself any hassles and some money by booking your accommodations a few weeks in advance of the trip. Waiting until closer to the trip risks losing out on lower ticket prices or housing options being limited.

3. Exchange your money for UK currency at your bank or credit union. Many places in the UK

do not accept any currency other than their official pound sterling (symbol: £) and you will need to exchange your money. Call, order online, or visit your local branch to see if your bank or credit union offers currency exchange. You may be able to avoid a fee if it's through your bank.

- Banks such as Bank of America, Chase, Citibank, and Wells Fargo offer currency exchange options. If you are not a member, you still might be able to take advantage of their exchange options for a fee.

- If you cannot exchange your currency before you depart, you will need to exchange it upon arrival. Be mindful that you will need to pay a fee to exchange your currency, and these can eat up your funds. There are several places to exchange money while in the UK, including bureaux de change (currency exchanges) in the airports and high streets, local banks, ATMs, and post offices.

- England, Scotland, and Northern Ireland issue their own pound sterling notes (paper bills) and coins. The English and Scottish pound sterling, with the exception of the Scottish £1, are accepted everywhere in the UK. The Northern Ireland pound sterling, however, is only accepted in Northern Ireland.

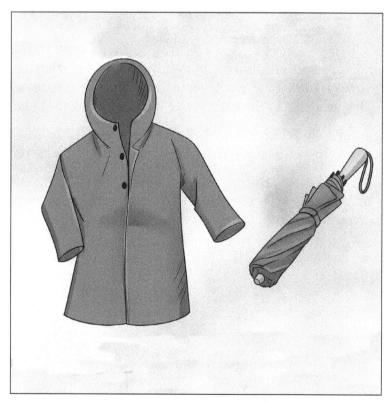

4. Pack for the weather. The weather in the UK is unpredictable as in many places, so make sure to pack an umbrella and other rain gear. Also pack for the season you are going: if it during the winter months in the UK, be mindful of how cold it can get and how early the daylight ends.

Part 4. Touring the UK

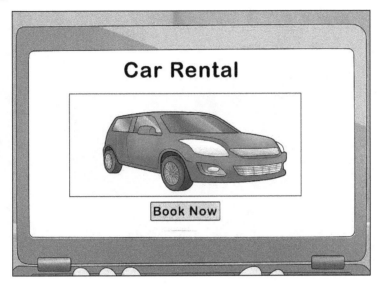

1. Arrange transport around the country. There are several different ways to get around the UK, including local public transit (subways, buses, and trollies), trains, travel buses, ferries, taxi, and car rentals. Research your transportation options for both local wandering around your lodging and longer commutes to your tourist destinations.

- If you booked a travel package, all of your transit to major tourist destinations might already be paid for. Check your itinerary to make sure.

2. See the sights. Visit the cities and towns that you planned to see and enjoy the travel experience. Don't be afraid to deviate away from the itinerary if the weather is not optimal or if another activity sounds more appealing. Take pictures of your favorite sights and look for other festivities during your downtime.

- Buy souvenirs as tokens of your travels if you find something you like. A tip is to buy useable souvenirs, like cups or blankets, or a collectable item like magnets.

3. Talk to the locals. Talking to local residents throughout your trip is a great way to learn about traditions, normal behaviors, lingo, food pairings, and what you can expect while exploring the UK.

- Ask about local traditions to learn more about the history of the area.

- Inquire about local shops and restaurants that might be worth a try.

- Making friends while in the UK is just another reason to go back.

Permissions

Index

Printed in the USA
CPSIA information can be obtained
at www.ICGtesting.com
JSHW051355091023
49903JS00006B/158